Avalanches

Titles in the Natural Disasters series include:

Natural **Disasters**

Avalanches

by Nathan Aaseng

Lucent Books
San Diego, California

Library of Congress Cataloging-in-Publication Data

Aaseng, Nathan, 1953–
    Avalanches / by Nathan Aaseng.
        p. cm. — (Natural disasters)
Includes bibliographical references and index.
Summary: A detailed description of avalanches which includes their types and causes as well as the prediction of their occurrence and techniques of survival afterwards.
    ISBN 1-56006-974-0 (hardback : alk. paper)
    1. Avalanches—Juvenile literature. [1. Avalanches.] I. Title. II. Natural disasters (Lucent Books)
    QC929.A8 A27 2002
    363.34'9—dc21

                                                    2001003334

Contents

Foreword

Fear and fascination are the two most common human responses to nature's most devastating events. People fear the awesome force of an earthquake, a volcanic eruption, a hurricane, and other natural phenomena with good reason. An earthquake can reduce multistory buildings to rubble in a matter of seconds. A volcanic eruption can turn lush forests and glistening lakes into a gray, flat landscape of mud and ash. A hurricane can lift houses from their foundations and hurl trucks and steel beams through the air.

As one witness to Hurricane Andrew, which hit Florida in 1992, recounts: "After the storm, planks and pieces of plywood were found impaling the trunks of large palms. . . . Eighteen-foot-long steel and concrete tie beams with roofs still attached were carried more than 150 feet. Paint was peeled from walls and street signs were sucked out of the ground and hurled through houses. Flying diesel fuel drums were a hazard, as were signs, awnings, decks, trash barrels, and fence posts that filled the skies. Mobile homes not only blew apart during the storm but disintegrated into aluminum shrapnel that became embedded in surrounding structures."

Fear is an understandable response to an event such as this, but it is not the only emotion people experience when caught in the throes of a natural disaster or when news of one blares from radios or flashes across television screens. Most people are fascinated by natural forces that have the power to claim life, crush homes, tear trees from their roots, and devastate whole communities—all in an instant. Why do such terrible events as these fascinate people? Perhaps the answer lies in humanity's inability to control them, and in the knowledge that they will recur—in some cases without warning—despite the scientific community's best efforts to understand and predict them.

A great deal of scientific study has been devoted to understanding and predicting natural phenomena such as earthquakes, volcanic eruptions, and hurricanes. Geologists and seismologists monitor the earth's motion from thousands of locations around the world. Their sensitive instruments record even the slightest shifts in the large tectonic plates that make up the earth's crust. Tools such as these have greatly improved efforts to predict natural disasters. When Mt. Pinatubo in the Philippines awoke from its six-hundred-year slumber in 1991, for example, a team of scientists armed with seismometers, tiltmeters, and personal computers successfully predicted when the volcano would explode.

Clearly, the scientific community has made great strides in knowledge and in the ability to monitor and even predict some of nature's most catastrophic events. Prediction techniques have not yet been perfected, however, and control of these events eludes humanity entirely. From the moment a tropical disturbance forms over the ocean, for example, researchers can track its progress and follow every twist in its path to becoming a hurricane but they cannot predict with certainty where it will make landfall. As one researcher writes: "No one knows when or where [a catastrophic hurricane] will strike, but we do know that eventually it will blast ashore somewhere and cause massive destruction. . . . Since there is nothing anyone can do to alter that foreboding reality, the question is: Are we ready for the next great hurricane?"

The many gaps in knowledge, coupled with the inability to control these events and the certainty that they will recur, may help explain humanity's continuing fascination with natural disasters. The Natural Disasters series provides clear and careful explanations, vivid examples, and the latest information about how and why these events occur, what efforts are being made to predict them, and to prepare for them. Annotated bibliographies provide readers with ideas for further research. Fully documented primary and secondary source quotations enliven the text. Each book in this series provides students with a wealth of information as well as launching points for further study.

Introduction

The White Death

Ulrike Schwartz arrived with her children in Galtür, Austria, in February 1999 expecting to enjoy the best skiing of her life. The German family had plenty of company. The week prior to their arrival more than three thousand tourists had flocked to this small village of seven hundred residents tucked away in a steep valley high in the Alps near the Swiss border. In the midst of one of the snowiest winters in memory, the slopes surrounding the internationally famous resort were covered in the type of deep, white powder that skiers dream about.

According to the experts, in fact, there was too much snow in the mountains. It had fallen so heavily and for so long that the roads to Galtür had been impassable all week. Austrian meteorologist Erhad Berger was among those warning that, under the current conditions, the risk of avalanches was terrifying. In all years prior to that winter, the avalanche danger had been rated at level-5—the highest possible danger—only three times. In February 1999 alone, sixteen level-5 warnings had been issued. Some government officials suggested that the town be evacuated.

Most of the residents and visitors of Galtür scoffed at the suggestion. The town was located 200 meters from the base of the mountain. Even a large avalanche would grind to a halt once it hit the valley bottom and would fall far short of the town. Although officials had spent $60 million on avalanche control in the Paznaum Valley where Galtür was nestled, the town itself was deemed so safe that authorities saw no reason to build protective avalanche barriers above it. On February 23 the town council voted not to implement an evacuation plan.

The relentless snowfall continued throughout the day. The Schwartz family spent the day relaxing in their chalet, waiting for the storm to let up before they returned to the slopes. Other tourists, such as Helmut and Christa Kapellner, wandered the streets of Galtür, shopping and taking pictures.

Meanwhile, high above them, the slopes were growing ever more dangerous. A furious wind had whipped the tons of snow into an enormous pile on the ridge above the valley. Then the temperature began to rise. A light rain added tons of weight to the snowpack.

Shortly after 4 P.M. two huge slabs of snow broke loose from the northwest slope of the valley. They merged to form a sliding 170,000-ton mass, 16 feet high and nearly 400 yards across, that threw a cloud of powder 200 yards into the air. The avalanche roared down the mountain, picking up speed and gathering more snow and debris as it fell. Within seconds a tidal wave of snow estimated at more than 350,000 tons

Overturned cars demonstrate the tremendous power of the avalanche that hit Galtür in Austria in 1999.

reached a speed of nearly 200 miles per hour, flattening trees and unearthing huge boulders.

The avalanche was so huge and powerful that, when it crashed to the floor of the Paznaun Valley, its momentum carried it to the town of Galtür. By the time the Kapellners, who had stopped to videotape the sights of Galtür, saw the awesome cloud bearing down on them, it was too late. The impact hurled Helmut more than 160 feet through the air, and he fell unconscious, struck by a falling roof. Christa found herself buried under a mountain of snow.

Meanwhile, the Schwartzes cringed in terror as the avalanche slammed into their chalet, blasted out the windows, and buckled the walls. "It was like looking into a swirling washing ma-

Residents of Galtür remove rubble and snow from buildings damaged by the avalanche.

chine,"[1] according to one observer. Ten chalets were completely destroyed in seconds. The avalanche overturned parked cars and swept them along for 60 meters.

Then, as suddenly as the onslaught struck, it was over. A village that had, only moments before, stood peacefully beneath the picturesque mountains was now virtually gone. Buildings were in shambles, and much of the town was entombed in a solid, dense whiteness. "That was not snow," marveled one of the shaken survivors. "It was like concrete."[2]

Frantically, those whom the avalanche had spared began digging to save those trapped in the snow. Although high winds kept outside rescue efforts from reaching the scene for sixteen hours, local rescuers dug out at least thirty living people. Among them was an unconscious Christa Kapellner, discovered after spending two hours encased in nearly 1.5 meters of snow beneath two cars. She recovered quickly, and the Schwartz family also escaped serious injury. But dozens of others were not so fortunate. Helmut Kapellner and thirty-one others, including eleven children, died.

The dreaded snow avalanche of the high mountains had claimed another set of victims. As has happened frequently throughout history, people had again underestimated the power and destruction of an event that outdoor experts have come to call the White Death.

Snow Falling Down Mountains

An avalanche is, at first glance, a very simple event. The term comes from an old French word, *avalanste*, which comes from *avaler*, meaning "to lower or let down." Basically, an avalanche is nothing more than the setting in motion of a large amount of temporarily stationary material that slides down a slope.

An avalanche can consist of solid material such as rocks, coal, or slag, the waste material from mining. In fact, such landslides are often the most destructive avalanches of all. In 1970 an earthquake triggered a gigantic rock avalanche in Peru, which claimed the lives of an estimated eighteen thousand people. Similarly, Canada's worst avalanche disaster came when ninety tons of limestone broke loose from the Turtle Mountains and destroyed the town of Frank, Alberta, killing ninety-five people.

But such disasters are freak accidents of nature or of human carelessness. The most common use of the term *avalanche* refers to an accumulation of snow; any other type of avalanche is classified as a special type, such as a rock or a mud avalanche. The standard definition of an avalanche, used in the rest of this book, is snow cover that falls or slides down a slope over a distance greater than 50 meters or 165 feet, about the width of a football field.

Common but Seldom Seen

Avalanches are among the most common of the devastating natural weather-related events. Experts estimate that at least 1 million of them take place every year. Although the vast majority occur during the winter, when snows are the heaviest, they can occur at any time of year in the high mountains, where snow is present year-round. Some of the most deadly avalanches have taken place on sunny summer days.

Despite the frequency of avalanches, relatively few people ever experience one. That is because they occur mainly in the bleakest, harshest, and least-populated placed places on Earth. Only a scattering of rugged souls ever venture into the deadly thin atmosphere of the Himalayas of Asia, the largest mountain chain in the world and the home of the most avalanches. Parts of the high Andes Mountains of South America and the Canadian Rockies are also virtually uninhabited. In the United States, where an estimated one hundred thousand avalanches occur each year, primarily in the Rockies, more than nine out of ten avalanches occur in places where no humans are present to witness them.

Avalanches are natural disasters that attract media attention only in the relatively rare cases in which they come into contact

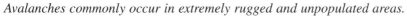

Avalanches commonly occur in extremely rugged and unpopulated areas.

with humans. This happens most frequently in the Alps of Europe, where the combination of steep mountains, high snowfall, and a sizable population living in high mountain valleys makes it the most likely location for avalanche damage. Whereas roughly two thousand avalanches are observed in the Rocky Mountains of Colorado each year, Switzerland reports between ten thousand and twelve thousand annually.

Types of Avalanches

Until little more than a century ago, most people thought of avalanches as giant snowballs that grew in mass and speed as they rolled down a snowfield. As Europeans became more familiar with them, they eventually realized that this was not the case. They divided avalanches into two types: dust avalanches, in which powdery snow swirled down a mountain, and ground avalanches, in which heavy snow slid along the ground.

In the 1930s mountaineers began making detailed studies of avalanches and discovered that these descriptions were not quite complete. After several decades of close observation, experts distinguished a wide variety of avalanches according to five criteria: the type of break, the position of the sliding surface, the humidity of the snow, the form of the track, and the form of movement.

The type of break is the most common characteristic that defines avalanches. The primary types of break are the loose-snow and the slab avalanches. Loose-snow avalanches form at or near the snow surface, often in fresh snow or very wet snow that does not hold together well. They begin at a point with a small amount of snow that dislodges more loose snow as it descends. The chain reaction of descending snow gives the avalanche the shape of an inverted V. Loose-snow avalanches are often dismissed as insignificant events commonly known as sluffs. They seldom contain enough snow to bury a person, cause injury, or inflict a great deal of property damage. Nonetheless, they are sometimes capable of sweeping a person off a cliff or against trees and rocks.

Slab avalanches are far more dangerous and cause the majority of avalanche fatalities. In a slab avalanche, the snowpack holds together until it is stressed to its breaking point, at which time the entire layer of snow falls at once in a devastating block. Slab avalanches can be further divided into soft slab and hard slab. The snowpack of a soft-slab avalanche builds up due to snowfall and is fairly loosely packed; a hard-slab avalanche is generally created by winds that drive the snow into a denser snowpack.

In addition to loose-snow and slab avalanches, several other types of breaks occur with less frequency. A glide avalanche results when trickling water loosens the snow

The dust avalanche (pictured) is characterized by powdery snow that swirls down a mountain.

from the ground, causing the entire snowpack to slide, sometimes for days, until it suddenly releases. An icefall avalanche occurs when a glacier—a permanent ice field—slowly flows downhill until it encounters a steep drop. Chunks of the glacier may then break off and fall. A cornice-fall avalanche is created when wind piles snow onto a ridge, forming an overhang of densely packed snow that may jut out many feet from the actual rock. This unsupported weight leaves it vulnerable to breaking off and tumbling down a slope.

Other Characteristics of Avalanches

The position of the sliding surface describes how much of the snow cover becomes a part of the avalanche. Some snowslides

A descending loose-snow avalanche formed near the snow's surface forms an inverted "V" shape.

are surface avalanches, in which only the top layer or top few layers of the snowpack break loose from the slope. In the more serious full-depth avalanches, many layers of snow are swept down in the slide.

Just as the amount of water can vary from snowfall to snowfall and between layers of snow cover, the humidity of avalanche snow can also vary. Wet avalanches are made up of melting snow or snow that has fallen at warm temperatures, and dry avalanches consist of snow that has fallen in cold weather or that has accumulated because of wind.

Avalanches differ with respect to the path they follow as they fall down a slope. A channeled avalanche is one in which the snow is directed or funneled by the land formation down a certain path. This type of avalanche takes place in canyons, gorges, or bowls. An unconfined avalanche occurs on open slopes, where it simply falls wherever gravity takes it.

Avalanches also differ in their forms of movement. When most people think of an avalanche, they think of a flowing avalanche that slides and tumbles down the surface of the slope. But in the airborne-powder avalanche, light, powdery snow flows down the slope suspended in the air. While this sounds quite harmless, an airborne-powder avalanche can cause tremendous damage. This kind of avalanche forms when the sudden collapse of the snow mass compresses the air in front of it so violently that, according to a *National*

Geographic writer, "the mass may rise and become airborne, and ride friction free on a cushion of air."[3] The force of the wind generated by the avalanche may reach speeds of over two hundred miles per hour. The powdery snowflakes kicked up by the avalanche form a suspension with a density that can be ten times greater than air.

When describing an avalanche, experts may refer to any or all of its characteristics. For example, a snowslide might be described as a flowing, channeled, wet-slab, depth avalanche.

Size Ratings

An avalanche can range from a small shift of a snow cover down a short slope to one dozens of feet deep that rumbles for miles, dropping several thousands of vertical feet from its starting point. The Canadian government has developed a system that divides avalanches into five classes according to the length of the fall and the amount of material contained in the slide. The rating system for avalanche size is similar to that used for earthquakes in that every advance in category signifies an event that is ten times greater than the previous level. A size-three avalanche, for example, is ten times larger than a size two and a hundred times larger than a size one.

Avalanches are divided into five classes according to length of fall and size.

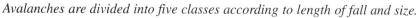

Size one describes an avalanche with a path of 33 feet that is relatively harmless to people, although one avalanche professional cautions, "In Utah, I saw a slide that had moved only 50 feet yet buried and suffocated a skier."[4] Size-two avalanches have a path in the 328-foot range and are considered a serious threat to bury, injure, or kill unprotected people in their paths. Size-three avalanches, with a 3,281-foot path, are capable of burying and demolishing an automobile, damaging a truck, breaking several trees, and destroying small buildings. A size-four avalanche may cover a 6,562-foot path. It can obliterate

In this channeled avalanche, snow is funneled by the natural shape of a mountain gorge.

The unconfined avalanche spreads outward on a mountain slope.

a large truck or railroad car, wipe out several buildings, and destroy a 10-acre forest. Size-five avalanches, the largest ever experienced, are capable of crushing an entire village or a 40-acre forest.

Human Encounters with Avalanches

For centuries the sudden fury with which avalanches could strike, the randomness of the destruction they caused, and the way they could instantly wipe out all traces of the victims convinced many people that avalanches were supernatural events. The Sherpas of the towering Himalayas of Nepal have long maintained a reverence for the mountains and the forces of nature that can strike with such fury. So terrified were Europeans of avalanches that they avoided climbing into the high mountains for fear of angering the terrifying forces that lived in them. Those who had to travel through mountain passes to their destinations did so quickly and in warm weather if at all possible. Folk legends arose and were passed from generation to generation, such as a popular riddle that went, "What flies without wings, strikes without hands, and sees without eyes? The avalanche beast."[5]

The first recorded mention of avalanches in literature is found in the writings of a Greek author named Strabo, from about 50 B.C. But there is evidence that approximately 170 years before this avalanches nearly wrecked one of the most famous military campaigns in history. In 218 B.C. the Carthaginian general Hannibal lost thousands of soldiers and horses while crossing the Alps to attack Rome, and avalanches are widely believed to have been responsible for many of the deaths.

Mountain Enterprises and Avalanches

Over the centuries rich mountain resources have lured adventurous—and often unsuspecting—people farther and farther into the paths of avalanches. Villages that sprang up in the beautiful high Alpine valleys could exist peacefully for many years before being surprised by an enormous avalanche. Although Native Americans seldom ventured into the high

The once peaceful Italian village of Ruinaux was obliterated by an avalanche in April 1914.

mountains during the winter, European trappers began inhabiting the high passes of the Rocky Mountains in search of winter pelts in the early nineteenth century. The discovery of precious metals in those same mountains in the middle of the nineteenth century attracted enterprising miners who understood little about sliding snowfields. Their ignorance and stubbornness made them ripe for horrific catastrophes.

The silver mining town of Alta, high in the Wasatch Mountains of northern Utah, provides a grim example of the price miners paid for their lack of avalanche awareness. In 1863 the newly built town was nearly wiped out by an avalanche and the fires that resulted when the sliding snowpack knocked over burning stoves used for cooking and heating. A decade later another avalanche cut loose from the high slopes of the Little Cottonwood Canyon and destroyed half the town, killing 60 people. Undeterred, the residents continued to play Russian roulette with the mountains. Ten years after the previous disaster, they lost again, as an avalanche swept through the town, killing 12. A year later yet another avalanche struck the town, taking 16 more lives. Researchers have tallied an avalanche death toll of 250 people in the Little Cottonwood Canyon area between 1865 and 1915. Gold miners in Colorado suffered a similar fate during that period. In the winter of 1883-1884 alone, over 100 prospectors died in avalanches in the Colorado Rockies.

As mining fizzled out in the mountains during the early part of the twentieth century, people departed the avalanche zones, and avalanche fatalities dropped significantly. For the next fifty years the major North American avalanche disasters occurred almost exclusively as a result of humans trying to force passage through treacherous mountain areas.

Two avalanches struck train routes in quick succession in the Rockies in 1910, making it the worst year by far in the history of North American avalanche disasters. In late February a series of snowslides bottled up two trains at the small station of Wellington, located near Steven's Pass high in the Cascade Mountains of Washington. While workers tried for a

Hannibal's Unseen Enemy

Historians consider Hannibal's assault on Rome in 218 B.C. to be one of the most daring and most spectacular military adventures of all time. The general from the ancient empire of Carthage conceded that his archenemy, Rome, held complete mastery of the sea. With the land routes to Rome from the west protected by the rugged Alps, this made a long-range attack on Rome nearly impossible.

Hannibal, however, was determined to try. He marched his army of roughly fifty thousand foot soldiers, nine thousand mounted soldiers, and three dozen elephants from the Spanish peninsula, across southern France, and into the Alps. Prior to this time no one had attempted to move such a large force through the Alps, even in good weather. For various reasons, Hannibal's expedition fell behind schedule and did not arrive in the Alps until well past September.

Beyond the fact that the army suffered terribly, information on exactly what happened in the Alps is sketchy. Most reports indicate that Hannibal emerged from the mountains with twenty to twenty-five thousand half-starved foot soldiers and six thousand horsemen. Reports vary about how the elephants fared. Avalanche experts such as McKay Jenkins and Colin Fraser, however, are convinced that avalanches accounted for a large share of the fatalities suffered.

week to clear the tracks, more avalanches bore down on them, burying and crushing entire train cars and shoving some of them over a cliff. The repeated avalanches also devastated the temporary shelters and outlying station buildings in which passengers and workers were holed up. Ninety-six people lost their lives in the pass, which made it by far the deadliest avalanche disaster in U.S. history.

Just four days later the Canadian Pacific Railroad sent a large contingent of workers to shovel out train tracks buried under an avalanche in Rogers Pass, British Columbia. While they were working, another gigantic avalanche crashed down on them, killing sixty-two workers.

Recreation and Avalanches

Such grim experiences brought an increased awareness of the danger of the White Death. Railroads took extra precautions to prevent such tragedies. This, along with the departure of miners from the mountains as the mines stopped yielding high-grade metal ore, made avalanche deaths in the United States extremely rare.

But after a brief period of abandonment, people discovered a new reason for entering the avalanche zones in ever greater numbers: Beginning in the middle of the eighteenth century, Europeans had finally overcome their terror of the high mountains and began climbing mountain peaks for sport. At first only a small handful of daring outdoor enthusiasts took to the sport of mountain climbing. But during the middle of the twentieth century, their numbers swelled.

Meanwhile, the sport of downhill skiing was growing out of its infancy into a flourishing industry. Introduced to the Alps in the late nineteenth century, this sport placed participants on the steep, wide-open slopes on which avalanches were most likely to occur. The first avalanche fatality involving skiers took place in the Alps in 1899. As the numbers of skiers increased, fatalities due to avalanches became an all-too-common tragedy, not only among skiers but also in the villages and chalets constructed in the high mountains to provide services to the skiers.

In the United States, where the steep mountains generally lay much farther from population centers than in Europe, skiing did not begin to catch on with the public until the 1930s. It was not until the 1950s and 1960s that a significant number of ski resorts were developed in the Rocky Mountains. As in Europe, the increase in mountain skiers during that time brought with it an increase in avalanche deaths.

During the 1970s and 1980s, backcountry skiing—the sport of skiing down mountains in remote areas far from ski resorts—attracted increasing numbers of enthusiasts. Lured by the thrill of skiing down slopes covered with deep powder snow untouched by human skis, backcountry skiers even took to

A Profile of Avalanche Victims

The vast majority of those who are killed or severely injured in avalanches are outdoor recreationists. In the five years between 1993 and 1998, thirty-five U.S. avalanche victims were snowmobilers, twenty-three were mountain climbers, fifteen were backcountry skiers, and ten were snowboarders. A few residents, hikers, workers, ski patrollers, field scientists, and motorists also lost their lives in freak avalanche accidents. Roughly 90 percent of the victims in the United States have been male, and most were between twenty and twenty-nine years of age. Almost all of them were well educated and were highly skilled at their sports, but they had little understanding of the nature of avalanches.

By bringing outdoor recreationists into previously inaccessible mountains, snowmobiles have changed the distribution of avalanche deaths. Until the late 1990s the majority of U.S. avalanche fatalities had occurred in Colorado, followed by Alaska, Washington, and Utah. In 2000–2001, however, Montana and Wyoming topped the fatality chart with seven apiece.

The winter sports enthusiast can become an unsuspecting victim in the path of an avalanche.

Although most avalanches take place during winter storms or immediately following them, few people are killed by avalanches during storms. The vast majority of victims are outdoors enjoying good winter weather. Fatal avalanche accidents most frequently occur when the sun is the highest, between noon and 2 P.M.

These British hikers in 1865 were among a growing number of Europeans who began climbing mountain peaks for sport.

having themselves transported by helicopter to otherwise inaccessible slopes. This brought increasing numbers of people into contact with avalanche-prone snowpacks.

In recent years snowmobiles have been newly designed with powerful engines and advanced technology that allow them to churn through deep snow and up steep mountain slopes. This has brought unprecedented numbers of recreationists into avalanche country. Between 1982 and 1998 the number of winter visitors to Wyoming's Yellowstone National Park more than doubled; over a third of the visitors to the area today are snowmobilers. One small town in the park played host to nearly fifty thousand snowmobilers in 1997 alone.

Deadlier than Ever

Since 1950 roughly 400 fatal avalanche accidents, resulting in nearly 600 deaths, have been documented in the United States. Between 1995 and 2000, more people were killed by avalanches in the United States than in any five-year period since 1950. Meanwhile, despite spending far more than the United States on avalanche education and prevention, Europe

The Worst U.S. Avalanche Disaster

Snow was falling so thickly in the Cascade Mountains of Washington that railroad workers fought a losing battle trying to keep the Great Northern Railway tracks open in February 1910. A total of eleven feet fell over the course of a few days, and in some places the tops of the telegraph poles barely poked through the surface.

Such snows blocked the tracks near Wellington Station so completely that two trains were trapped, unable to move in either direction. Their situation was made even more precarious by the ignorance of the railroad crews about avalanches. They had clear-cut the forest on the slopes above the town to provide fuel and construction materials. Now, unimaginable depths of snow piled above Wellington with nothing to help hold them in place.

Late on the night of February 24 a small avalanche broke loose and destroyed a cook shed, killing two men. The avalanche snow, added to the fallen and drifted snow, sealed the trains in even tighter. Plows were stopped in their tracks by a dense, thirty-five-foot-deep avalanche runout filled with tree stumps and other debris.

The slow work of digging out the trains continued for several days, interrupted periodically by more small avalanches. On February 27 the weather turned warm. Snow changed to sleet and then to rain by the next morning. Late that night, during an electrical storm, a huge slab nearly a quarter of a mile wide broke off the mountain slope. According to one witness, quoted in McKay Jenkins's *The White Death*, "Relentlessly it advanced, exploding, roaring, rumbling, grinding, snapping—a crescendo of sound that might have been the crashing of a thousand freight trains." The avalanche pushed an entire train off a ledge into a canyon and shattered structures such as a water tower and an engine house.

The survivors searched and dug frantically in a driving rain. They rescued a total of twenty-two more survivors, but ninety-six others lost their lives.

Railroad officials realized too late the folly of putting so many people in the path of such massive avalanches. Both the town and the route were abandoned. Great Northern bored an eight-mile tunnel lower on the mountain and relocated the track to this safer location.

Skiers find enjoyment on a backcountry slope despite the danger of avalanches in these areas.

witnessed the deaths of 1,200 people on its slopes during the 1980s alone. Currently the death toll due to avalanches in the Alps hovers around 150 per year.

The injury and fatality statistics on avalanches reflect the growing numbers of outdoor enthusiasts who choose high-risk avalanche zones as their playgrounds. In 1954 and 1955 the United States reported no fatalities due to avalanches. As the popularity of ski resorts and mountain climbing grew in the 1960s, avalanche deaths averaged about five per year. The increase in backcountry skiing was most responsible for pushing the death toll to an average of fifteen per year during the 1970s. During the late 1990s snowmobiles helped trigger a rise in the average number of avalanche fatalities to nearly thirty per year. Prior to 1994 no more than two snowmobilers had died in avalanche accidents in any one year. During the next five years thirty-five snowmobilers lost their lives in avalanches. In the winter of 2000–2001 alone, avalanches accounted for forty deaths in the United States and Canada. The bottom line is that avalanches represent a greater threat than ever before.

What Causes an Avalanche?

For many centuries and in many cultures, people associated the sudden, terrifying onslaught of rolling, isolated snowstorms with angry gods, evil demons or monsters, and even the practice of the dark arts. A trial in Switzerland in 1652 concluded authoritatively that "witches are the causes of avalanches,"[6] and there are other documented instances of people being put to death on suspicion of having conjured up an avalanche.

The eerie randomness of avalanches' destruction helped reinforce the notion that mysterious forces were behind these occurrences. For example, one powerful avalanche in 1806 tore up a large section of forest in the Alps, but the hurtling mass of snow and tree trunks sailed over a nearby village without causing any harm. There was, however, a spectacular reminder of the near miss: A single tree trunk embedded itself and stood straight up in the roof of a pastor's house. The locals could not help but think some mysterious force had deliberately spared the village and placed the tree in that peculiar spot.

Beginning in the middle of the twentieth century, however, investigators took a scientific approach to the study of avalanches. They have determined that avalanches are a creation of heavy snowfall, steeply angled slopes, and instability in the bonds between snow crystals.

Heavy Snow, Steep Slopes

The first two of these requirements—heavy snowfall and steeply angled slopes—would seem to be laughably obvious.

However, avalanches would not be such a common occurrence if mountains had the same snowfall conditions that exist in most localities around the world. It is a fact of nature that snow falls most heavily in the mountains. This happens because heavy storm clouds that are unable to rise up past the height of the mountains get stuck and remain stationary while they release their precipitation. Portions of the Canadian Rockies and Glacier National Park in the United States regularly receive as

Sudden heavy snowfalls create likely environments for avalanches.

much as eighty feet of snow per year. It is not uncommon for such places to accumulate several feet of snow in a single day. Although other mountain ranges do not experience quite this extreme in snow levels, all tend to acquire enormous piles of snow such as are seldom seen at lower altitudes. These deep piles of snow provide the raw material of avalanches.

The requirement of steep slopes seems similarly obvious. Eighty-foot-deep blankets of snow would be of little consequence if they accumulated on a plain or on rolling hills. Similarly, however, avalanches cannot occur on mountain faces that are so steep that falling snow cannot adhere to their surfaces. Researchers have discovered that 98 percent of all avalanches take place on slopes of between twenty-five and fifty degrees, and 90 percent occur on slopes between thirty and forty-five degrees. The most common slope angle for avalanches is thirty-five degrees.

Snow Binding

Just because heavy snow accumulates on a steep slope does not mean that an avalanche is likely. The most crucial, and least understood, factor in the creation of an avalanche is the stability of the snowpack. The task of studying snow stability has not been easy, for, as Monty Atwater, one of the world's most experienced avalanche researchers, observes, "Snow seems averse to being studied. When it is poked or disturbed or manhandled in any way, it changes quicker than a chameleon, from one kind of snow to another, leaving observers baffled."[7]

Nonetheless, researchers have found out a great deal about snow stability. Basically, stability refers to the tendency of the snow crystals to stick together and withstand the force of gravity that pulls them downward. The shape of snowflakes or snow crystals, of which there may be 10 million in a cubic foot of snow, can vary vastly depending on weather conditions. Experts identify many types of snow crystal shapes, such as needles, columns, plates, stellars, and hail. Each of these different forms has different bonding capabilities. Snow crystal forms such as hail do not bind together well, but plate crystals are more cohesive. In addition, the water content of snow can vary. A cubic foot of very cold, dry snow may contain as little as 5 percent of its volume in water whereas a warm, wet snow may be 50 percent water. Wet snow tends to stick better than dry snow.

Along with water content and crystal shape, weather conditions can impact the ability of the snow crystals to bind together. Cold and warm temperatures can alter the shape of the crystals and their binding power. For example, crystals bind most easily at temperatures close to the melting point of snow. This fact can be confirmed by anyone trying to make snowballs: At colder temperatures the snow does not stick together. Furthermore, wind compacts the snow, causing it to bind differently than snow falling on a calm day.

The stability of a snow bank helps to determine the potential of an avalanche occurring.

A Bad Foundation

The binding characteristics of snow continue to change as the snow lies on the ground. Over time fallen snow tends to break into smaller, simpler, and more densely packed crystals. In most cases, water vapor moves between the snow crystals and forms bridges between them that cause the snow to hold together. As each layer is compressed by the weight of the snow above, it becomes thinner, denser, and more tightly packed, like cement. This type of snow is quite stable and, by itself, has little potential to form an avalanche. The layer of snow will generally hold together so well that it becomes elastic—

that is, it may be pulled and stretched downhill by the force of gravity without breaking.

Snow that falls at a slow rate is far less likely to cause an avalanche than snow that falls thickly and accumulates quickly. As world-reknowned mountaineer and ice-climbing expert Yvon Chouinard says, "A heavy snowfall spread out over a few days may not be dangerous since settling will often stabilize the snow faster than it can build up."[8] Heavy snows in a short period of time, on the other hand, may build up to dangerous levels well before the snowfall has a chance to settle and stabilize.

Researchers have found, however, that the ability of individual snowflakes to bind to each other is not as important as the binding that occurs between snowfall layers. A stable early snowpack provides a firm foundation for later snows to bond well and hold together. Yet the most stable, cohesive layer of snow may create a serious avalanche threat if the layer underneath it is unstable. "It's kind of like building a house on a bad foundation,"[9] explains Clair Israelson, a Canadian public safety specialist. In fact, snow crystals that bond well with other crystals within a layer may form a deeper and more dangerous snowpack than poorly bonding snow.

Late in winter a mountain slope may hold dozens of layers of snowfall, each from a different snowstorm. All it takes to send a cascade of snow sliding is for a small amount of pressure to be applied to a snowpack in which one of the layers is unstable. Avalanche experts have concluded that slightly more than nine out of ten avalanche accidents occur on slopes where a weakly bonded layer lies deep in the snowpack.

Unstable Snow Layers

An incredible variation in the types of snow can be found in different layers on a single slope. Among the types that are the least stable are depth-hoar, surface-hoar, extreme-temperature, fluffy, and sun-crusted snow.

Depth-hoar snow, sometimes called sugar snow, is an extremely unstable snowpack condition that forms when the ground is still fairly warm but the air is cold. The warm air from the ground creates water vapor in the fallen snow. This vapor rises upward, where it meets the colder air and tends to freeze onto the edges of existing snow crystals. As it does so, it changes the crystals into coarse grains with sharp angles. This creates a type of snow that does not bond to other snow even under great pressure. This layer of depth-hoar snow is usually separated from the new snow that falls on it by a thin, fragile crust. This crust can often hold a great deal of snow, but if it breaks, the result is colorfully described by experts as letting loose a pile of ball bearings or marbles. The top, stable layers of snow slide "like bricks on potato chips."[10] Depth-hoar snow becomes an even greater threat during major thaws.

Avalanches like this one at Ruth Glacier in Alaska result from unstable snow layers that break apart.

As it becomes wet, it loses what little binding ability it had and takes on a form commonly referred to as rotten snow.

Depth-hoar snow is commonly found in areas such as the Rockies, where the snow tends to be cold and dry. It is especially dangerous because it typically occurs early in the winter, in October or November, and thereby creates an unstable base for the deep snows that follow throughout the entire winter.

Another highly unstable snowpack layer is surface-hoar snow, which forms on winter slopes in much the same way as dew forms on grass in warmer weather. As the temperature drops at night, the air loses its ability to hold moisture and some of it precipitates onto the snow. There, it freezes into feathery crystals that bind poorly, thus forming a thin layer of extremely slippery ice.

Extremes in weather temperatures, whether cold or warm, also create a great deal of snowpack instability. Snow falling in very cold temperatures tends to form needle-shaped crystals that bind poorly with other snow. Snow falling in warm temperatures may take the form of ice granules, which do not bind, or sleet, which forms treacherously slippery surfaces. Warm temperatures also may cause melting that may weaken the bonds between snow layers. Even on fairly cool days, bright sunshine can melt snow at the surface of the snowpack. When the sun goes down, the melted snow refreezes, creating a thin, slick surface—similar to surface-hoar snow—that does not hold snow well.

The distribution of weight in the snowpack can also play a role in snowpack stability. A combination of light, fluffy snow followed by thick layers of heavy snow may create a top-heavy snowpack that needs only the slightest of triggers to set it sliding downhill. Sudden changes in weather are one cause of this potentially dangerous condition. As Chouinard ex-

Loud Noises and Avalanches

The notion that loud noises can trigger avalanches has been around for centuries. Avalanche expert Colin Fraser writes in *Avalanches and Snow Safety* that when Napoléon led his French army through the Alps during 1800, one of his generals issued an urgent decree: "No one is to cry or call out for fear of causing a fall of avalanches."

Despite its longevity, however, the widespread belief has no basis in fact. In the late 1940s Monty Atwater tested the theory and found that although certain sound vibrations can trigger avalanches, sound volume has virtually no effect. Bruce Tremper, director of the Utah Avalanche Forecasting Center, says that noises trigger avalanches "only in the movies. In 20 years as an avalanche professional, I have never once seen an avalanche triggered by, say a shout, even a sonic boom or low-flying helicopter. It's just not enough force."

plains, "A snowfall starting with cold temperatures and dry snow and followed by warmer temperatures is likely to cause avalanches because the dry snow on the bottom is not likely to bond to the old snow, and the new, denser snow on top will result in an unstable 'top-heavy' condition."[11]

Additional Weight

Heavy snows place pressure on the bonds that keep the snowpack in place against the pull of gravity. Even the most stable snowpack tends to be compressed and stretched by the weight of additional snow accumulating on it, and it will creep and slide downhill. An avalanche results when some weakness in one or more of the snowpack layers causes the snowpack to break under this pressure. The more unstable the layers in the snowpack, the less pressure is required to set it off. Any additional weight piled on an unstable snowpack, therefore, increases the chances that the snowpack will break and an avalanche will occur.

Every snowfall piles more weight on the snowpack. The heavier it snows, the greater the pressure on the snowpack and the greater the danger of an avalanche. Gently falling snow adds this new weight so gradually that the snowpack is often able to adjust to the increased load and restabilize without triggering an avalanche. Snow falling at a rate faster than one inch per hour, however, builds up weight faster than the snow can settle. The addition of a significant blanket of weight to a snowfield, whether caused by snowfall or wind, is the primary factor in creating potential avalanche situations. Roughly 80 percent of all avalanches occur during or shortly after a storm or high winds.

The pressure that new snow exerts on a snowpack is a major determining factor in the formation of avalanches. However, snowfall is not the only way in which precarious weight is added to snowfields. Chouinard explains that high wind commonly "scours snow off the windward slopes, pulverizes it, and drops it off on the leeward side."[12]

According to the Association of American Avalanche Professionals, wind can deposit snow in a particular area ten times faster than falling snow. The compacting force of wind is so great that this windblown snow may also be many times denser than fallen snow. Both of these factors means that high winds can load a snow-packed hillside with a tremendous amount of dense snow in a short period of time, creating a highly unstable situation.

Sometimes windblown snow forms cornices on ridges and rock outcroppings. The snow piled on a cornice may jut far out from the rocks in a tightly compressed cone with no ground directly beneath it—becoming extremely unstable.

Terrain Factors

In addition to snow accumulation and steep slopes, the terrain is a factor in determining the likelihood of an avalanche. Even in snow layers that bind poorly with other layers, a snowpack may remain stable if other objects hold it in place. Thickly forested slopes, for example, provide many anchors for the snowpack. Large boulders or rock outcroppings offer the

Windblown snow on rock outcroppings often forms unstable cornices.

Trees and boulders offer support by holding snow in place or by break-ing the momentum of an avalanche.

same support. Trees and boulders can also serve as brakes that stop or slow the momentum of a snowslide before it can build up to a dangerous level.

On the other hand, a long, open stretch of ground provides no anchors. This can result in a domino effect in which a very small break in the snow cover sets off a chain reaction that engulfs an entire slope.

It is the lack of tree cover that makes the Alps particularly vulnerable to large avalanches. The tree line is lower in the Alps than in most mountain ranges, meaning that the mountain slopes lie bare and exposed at relatively low altitudes. This situation has been compounded in past centuries by the cutting down of forests in the Alps for wood products.

Mountains Full of Snow

Snowfall is more difficult to measure than rainfall because wind, settling, and melting can all distort the figures. Nonetheless, snowfall figures have been recorded in many locations for decades. They show that mountains are, far and away, the snowiest places on Earth.

The greatest snowfall in a single season was recorded during the winter of 1998–99 at an elevation of 4,200 feet on Mount Baker in northwestern Washington. Official measurements place the total at 1,140 inches. The heaviest snowfall over a 24-hour period was the 74 inches that landed on Silver Lake, Colorado, on April 14–15, 1921. Bessen, France, received almost as much snow: 68 inches in just 19 hours on April 5–6, 1969. The greatest snowstorm in history took place at Mount Shasta, California. Beginning on February 13, 1959, the storm raged until February 19, dumping 189 inches of snow before the skies cleared.

Contrasting these figures, the typical snowfall of even some of the U.S. cities noted for their severe winters is hardly worth mentioning. The average annual snowfall in Chicago is 39 inches; Minneapolis, Minnesota 50 inches; and Anchorage, Alaska, 70 inches. Even Buffalo, New York, famous for the heavy snows that blow off Lake Erie, receives only 92 inches in a typical winter.

An avalanche scours a mountain in Evolene, Switzerland.

Avalanche Triggers

Because unstable layers of snow can form under so many conditions, the mountains of the world are filled with huge snowfields clinging precariously to steeply angled slopes. Given this situation, avalanche expert Monty Atwater observes, "To me, the mystery has never been that it [snow] avalanches but that it usually stays on the mountains so well."[13] In many cases the snowpack is so unstable that the slightest addition of weight at a single point can trigger a devastating snowslide.

Most often, it is the addition of new snow that not only creates a potential avalanche situation but actually triggers the avalanche itself. At some point, the snowfield is no longer able to support the increasing pressure caused by the weight of the new snow, particularly wet snow. The bonds holding the snow in place will break, and the snow mass will submit to the force of gravity.

Similarly, warm weather may cause melting that weakens the bonds between snow layers. Even a snowpack that has been relatively stable for weeks can be overwhelmed by the pressure of heavy snowfall, particularly wet snow, and spring rains that cause it to suddenly break loose. In the Himalayas, the tremendous altitude creates an alternating combination of intense sunshine during the day and bitter temperatures at night. The slippery surfaces created by the melting-freezing cycles produce avalanches with virtually every storm.

Although relatively infrequent, falling cornices have triggered a number of major avalanches. The densely packed snow of a cornice, falling from a great height onto a snowfield, can strike with such a devastating impact that it can jar even a relatively stable snowfield loose from its moorings.

Human Triggers

Any added weight or stress on an unstable snowfield can trigger an avalanche. A wild animal crossing an unstable slope could trigger an avalanche, although documentation of such an event is virtually unknown. Human triggering of avalanches, however, is well documented. For although most avalanches are triggered by snowfall or melting, few of those avalanches are ever seen, much less experienced, by people. Fully 95 percent of the avalanche accidents involving humans are triggered either by the victims or someone in their party.

Since 1950 skiers have been responsible for most of the human-triggered avalanches. But in the United States during the 1990s, snowmobilers were primarily responsible for providing the extra pressure needed to break up unstable snowfields. In *The Insiders' Guide to Glacier*, Eileen Gallagher notes, "Snowmobilers are at the greatest risk because their

Human Triggers

The vast majority of avalanche victims bring disaster to themselves through their own ignorance or errors of judgment. One hiker in Colorado's Rocky Mountain National Park described how he was caught in a situation he should have seen coming. In an article entitled "Buried Alive," which appeared in *Discover*, Winston Cheyney writes that while trudging up a slope after a friend, "I was having a hard time getting into his steps because I'd step up into a step and then when I put my weight on it, I'd break into some real soft sugar snow underneath. And I didn't put two and two together." Seconds later, as his friend froze in horror only a few yards away, he found himself engulfed in a terrifying avalanche that he had set off.

Five snowboarders looking for thrills in northern Utah serve as prime examples of why clueless recreationists and deep mountain snows are a poor mix. The first major snowstorm of the season brought the impatient snowboarders to the Wasatch Mountains on November 7, 1998, even though the ski resorts were not yet open. Reveling in the fun of having two feet of fresh powder snow on the slopes all to themselves, the first four zoomed down one of the slopes, apparently with no ill effects. The fifth young man, however, pushed the limits of the unstable slope too far and triggered a small avalanche, perhaps fifty feet wide. The slide pushed the snowboarders off a cliff and tumbled them five hundred feet down the mountain. When the snow clouds cleared, the man who had triggered the slide was nowhere to be seen. His body was found three hours later deep in the snow only twenty feet from where his surviving friends had ended up.

Snowmobilers sometimes trigger avalanches in backcountry, avalanche-prone areas.

powerful machines can carry them into the highest and most avalanche-prone reaches."[14] Mountain climbing, snowboarding, and hiking are other activities that commonly set off avalanches. In the vast majority of cases, those who triggered the avalanche failed to heed some of the basic warning signs that should have alerted them to the danger. "The people out recreating only feel the stuff on top," observes Clair Israelson. "They can't appreciate that those weak layers are down there hiding."[15]

Predicting
Avalanches

Once avalanche experts determined the conditions that create potential avalanche situations, predicting avalanches became a relatively simple matter of recognizing those conditions. In response to avalanche disasters in the past, many governments in mountainous areas have set up avalanche centers to constantly evaluate avalanche conditions and alert the public of possible dangers. Public financing of avalanche forecasting centers has been increasing in the Alps since the first programs were started there during the 1950s. Presently, the most popular winter recreation areas throughout the world provide information on avalanche conditions to visitors. The Yellowstone Avalanche Center in Wyoming, for example, employs two full-time and one part-time avalanche expert to keep a close watch on conditions in the area.

In addition, the skiing and outdoor recreation industries, which have a large stake in preventing recreation disasters, have taken an active interest in avalanche forecasting. Ever since budget cuts forced the U.S. Forest Service to eliminate its avalanche research center in Fort Collins, Colorado, in the 1980s, a cooperative effort of the ski industry and the Colorado Department of Transportation has helped fill the void by funding the Colorado Avalanche Information Center in Boulder.

Official Warnings

Avalanche conditions are monitored closely in most of the mountainous regions that support significant populations or host large numbers of outdoor recreationists. In the most popular ski areas, avalanche conditions are updated around the clock. Utah's avalanche centers, for example, issue hourly updates on avalanche conditions in the Wasatch Mountains, a prime ski area. On a smaller scale, ski resorts and outdoor recreation centers constantly evaluate the local avalanche danger for their clients.

North American officials have developed a color-coded system for quickly classifying avalanche danger. Green signifies low avalanche danger. Outdoor activity in a green area is generally considered to be safe. Yellow stands for moderate danger. In a yellow area, there is little threat of a naturally occuring avalanche. However, recreationists and travelers are advised that there is a chance of human-triggered avalanches and caution is advised on slopes that have the features of likely avalanche terrain. Orange signifies considerable avalanche danger. Under

A sign at Glacier National Park in Montana warns of an extreme danger of an avalanche occurring.

such conditions, unstable slabs of snow probably exist on steep slopes. Avalanches due to natural causes on such slopes are possible, and if humans go there it is probable that they will trigger an avalanche. Red means high avalanche danger. Travel into a red avalanche zone is not recommended. It means that unstable slabs probably exist on a variety of terrains and both natural and human-triggered snowslides are likely. Finally, black stands for extreme avalanche danger. This means that unstable slabs exist on most slopes, and that widespread avalanches are certain to occur in the area within the next few hours. Large, devastating avalanches are possible, and people are strongly advised to stay out of the area.

There is no one test or technique that experts use in evaluating the potential for avalanches. A combination of weather analysis, knowledge of the terrain, and field observations is required to give an accurate picture of conditions on the mountains.

Weather Reports

Since more than 85 percent of all avalanches occur within twenty-four hours of a significant snowfall, snow reports are one of the most common indicators of avalanche potential. But high winds and rapidly changing weather can also play an important role in setting up avalanche conditions. Thorough avalanche assessment requires not only an understanding of the current weather conditions but also of those that existed in previous weeks and the conditions that are expected in the near future. Measurements of snowfall totals, wind speeds, extreme fluctuations in temperature, the amount of rain falling on new snow, and the presence of a warm sun beating down on the snow can provide clues about the snow conditions that presently exist. But knowledge of the pattern of snowstorms during the current winter season is required to understand the makeup of the current snowpack and how it might be affected by various weather changes. And because snowpack conditions can change rapidly, accurate weather forecasts are important for anyone venturing into a mountain wilderness area. "Every single time one ventures out into the hills in winter," writes Bill Birkett, author of *Modern Rock and Ice Climbing*, "it is essential to know the weather forecast and be prepared accordingly."[16]

Unfortunately, not all sources of weather reports are completely reliable. During the devastating 1998–1999 avalanche season in the Alps, resort owners and town officials repeatedly downplayed the seriousness of the dangerous snowfalls and temperature conditions in the mountains in an effort to keep tourists from canceling their reservations. "What you and I read in the newspaper about snowfall may be somewhat of a public relations person's dream designed to attract skiers," warns Alan Dennis, a Canadian avalanche control manager. He advises outdoor recreationists to check with official weather and avalanche sources, such as the Canadian Avalanche Centre in Revelstoke, British Columbia. "What we get here is the technical goods—the real stuff,"[17] he explains.

Local Familiarity

Current weather reports can be combined with the past history of an area to provide a reasonable guess about the general avalanche conditions. Some regions and specific slopes are

No Rule of Thumb

In countries where large populations live in known avalanche fields, experts have used advanced technology to predict the likely path of avalanches. The town of Flateyri, Iceland, for example, compiled computer-generated maps of known avalanche slides to predict danger and to avoid building where the threat was the greatest. Yet despite all of this preparation, in November 1995 a gigantic avalanche rumbled toward Flateyri down a path that had never before been taken by an avalanche or predicted by computer. The slide, weighing a quarter of a million tons, caught the town off guard and killed twenty people.

Similarly, the fatal avalanche that struck Galtür traveled a route that most forecasters had not expected. Such incidents reinforce the fact that the science of avalanches is far from complete.

A sign alerts skiers of an avalanche-prone area.

notorious for producing avalanches, and it may be expected that under certain weather conditions these areas will pose high risks for anyone living in or traveling through them. Familiarity with the ways in which the local climate affects the snowpack is also important in assessing avalanche potential. Experienced avalanche analysts know that snowfall in the Cascade Mountains of Washington is likely to be heavy and wet while snowfall in Colorado's Rocky Mountains tends to be lighter and drier, and they take these differences into account when analyzing the effect of weather conditions.

Knowledge of the peculiarities of the local climate is especially important in areas such as Asia's Himalayas, where the altitudes are far higher than other places on Earth. For example, experienced mountaineer Yvon Chouinard notes that the Himalayas' unique combination of intense sunlight and cold temperatures means that "timing is the key to safe movement in these mountains."[18] According to Chouinard, if there is precipitation in the Himalayas at night, avalanches can be expected to occur at about nine or ten o'clock in the morning, when the sun has had a chance to destabilize the snowpack. If snow falls during relatively warm days, snowslides can be expected to take place after the sun sets and falling temperatures cause the destabilization.

Detailed knowledge of the local terrain is also important in forecasting avalanche danger. "The person who knows the country remembers the location of a rock slide or a cut-down forest,"[19] advises Chouinard. Such features offer clues that a particular slope is especially susceptible to avalanches.

Field Observation

Although weather reports and familiarity with local conditions can give a general idea of what avalanche conditions may be like, there is no substitute for on-the-spot observation. Veteran avalanche professional Bruce Tremper insists that dangerous avalanche slopes "almost always have obvious signs."[20] Virtually all of these signs can be recognized,

Mountaineers watch as an avalanche tumbles toward their camp in the Himalayan mountains in Nepal.

not only by experts but also by trained recreationists and others traveling into avalanche territory.

A great deal of useful information can be gained simply by observing a slope. One of the most basic measures of avalanche potential in a given area is the angle of the slope. This can be quickly determined by using an inexpensive instrument known as a slope meter. Measurements with a slope meter will reveal whether a slope is within the thirty- to forty-five-degree range that is the prime avalanche angle.

The direction that a slope faces can also be a factor. South-facing slopes get the full effect of sunlight while north-facing slopes may be in shadows much of the winter. The difference this causes in local weather conditions can be surprising. In the Northern Hemisphere, north-facing slopes tend to produce more frequent and larger avalanches during midwinter; south-facing slopes tend to be more hazardous during the spring.

The direction of the slope also influences the effect of wind. In the United States, where the prevailing winds come from the west, western slopes are less likely to pose avalanche problems. This is because the wind scours the snow off of these slopes and deposits it in areas where the wind is blocked.

Since dense, windblown snow tends to be especially dangerous, snowdrifts are good indicators of potential avalanche problems, regardless of the direction of the slope. The appearance of large cornices along the ridges provides evidence that high winds have produced a great deal of potentially dangerous drifting in the area.

The surface of the snowpack may also provide clues about the stability of the slope. Cracks or fissures running along the surface of the snow are examples of small breaks in the bonds that hold the snow together. They are a strong indication of weakness in one or more of the snow layers.

Vegetation and Terrain

A survey of the vegetation and terrain of a slope reveals important information about avalanche potential. The most ob-

Wrong Place, Wrong Time

Russian climber Vladimir Shatayev points out that although all reasonable safety precautions should be taken during any winter mountain adventure, risk is always involved. "Safe mountains do not exist," says Shatayev in his book *Degrees of Difficulty*.

Even the top experts in the world sometimes find themselves at the mercy of the elements when they happen to be in the wrong place at the wrong time. On April 12, 1964, Bud Werner, a top U.S. skier, was killed in an avalanche while shooting a film at St. Moritz, Switzerland. In July 1974 a top U.S. mountain climbing team scaling Lenin Peak in the Soviet Union ran into a freak disaster. While the group was on the mountain, two separate earthquakes triggered freak avalanches. One of them landed on the tent of expert climbers Bob Craig and Gary Ullin. Their teammates were able to dig out Craig, but Ullin did not survive. "It was possible what would then occur had not happened for a thousand years, and would not for another thousand, but it happened to them," writes Shatayev.

In 1998 world-famous Russian mountain climber Anatoli Boukreev died scaling the 26,700-foot peak of Annapurna in the Himalayas when a falling cornice triggered a massive avalanche that he could not avoid. A year later another Himalayan avalanche buried and killed Alex Lowe, widely regarded as the finest all-around mountaineer in the world.

For bad luck, however, nothing can top the fate of a large group of climbers scaling Mount Rainier's Ingraham Glaciers. In a bizarre case of being in the wrong place at the wrong time, eleven people in the party of twenty-two died when they were crushed by an enormous block of ice that broke free above them.

vious clues are evidence of recent snowslides. Fallen or broken trees, displaced rocks and vegetation; stretches of loose, unpacked snow; and piles of snow at the bottom of a slope all indicate that an avalanche has recently occurred. Conditions that are favorable for one avalanche have a good chance of spawning others. In fact, avalanches often occur in series, with one snowslide after another rushing down the same unstable slope.

The presence of a large number of intact trees and outcroppings of rock, on the other hand, tends to indicate a fairly stable slope since these objects anchor the snowpack. It is extremely rare for a natural avalanche to start in a dense forest or among large projections of rocks. In order to be effective anchors, however, trees and rocks must be closely spaced. A sparse stand of trees has only a small effect on the stability of a slope. Steep, heavily drifted slopes above the tree line, where there is nothing to help hold the snowpack together, present the most dangerous avalanche conditions, particularly after a recent snow or high winds.

Field observation can also provide clues about whether a recent snowfall has had time to settle and stabilize. One U.S. government avalanche organization advises looking at tree branches. "If the trees are still holding snow after a storm," says the National Forest Service's Manti LaSal Avalanche Forecasting Center, "one might surmise that the snow on the ground has not had a chance to settle either."[21]

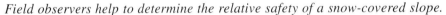

Field observers help to determine the relative safety of a snow-covered slope.

Assessing the Danger

Field observation not only can reveal clues about the likelihood of
an avalanche, it can also warn of
areas in which a snowslide is
likely to produce the most severe
consequences. For example, an
unstable slope dotted with a
sparse stand of trees and a few isolated boulders can be more dangerous than a slope with no
vegetation. This is because these
objects can be swept up in an
avalanche and come hurtling
down the mountain, causing injury and death; an avalanche on a
clear slope would not have posed
such a danger. Slopes that become
steeper farther downhill from an
unstable snowfield present an in-

*Tree branches, rocks, and other objects swept
up in an avalanche could cause serious injury.*

creased danger because an avalanche can gain momentum and
thus pack a more powerful punch on such terrain.

Experienced avalanche professionals also pay close attention to what is at the bottom of a slope. If the slope ends at a
steep cliff, a person caught in even a minor snowslide may be
whisked off the edge and dashed against rocks hundreds of
feet below. If a stand of trees or a pile of rocks is at the bottom of a smooth slope, a person caught in a fast-moving
avalanche may be slammed against this barrier, sustaining
equally lethal injuries.

One of the most important terrain features that impacts on
the danger of an avalanche is the configuration of the slope. A
short slope that is narrow at the top and widens at the bottom
may not pose a serious danger if it avalanches because the
snow will tend to disperse as it slides. A long slope that is
wide at the top or middle and narrows toward the bottom is
especially hazardous because the snow funnels into one spot,

which concentrates it into a large, lethal mass. Equally dangerous is a concave, or bowl-shaped, slope in which the edges of the slope are higher than the middle. Not only does the bowl-shaped slope funnel snow toward the middle, but it also tends to serve as a catch basin for accumulating staggering amounts of snow.

Testing the Snowpack

Although weather reports, experience, and field observations can provide valuable general clues for predicting the likelihood of an avalanche, avalanche experts know better than to rely on them completely. "Looking at a snowy slope can't tell you if it's safe,"[22] say the authors of *The Insiders' Guide to Yellowstone*. The most valuable indicators of avalanche potential lie in the composition of the snowpack.

There are two basic methods of evaluating the stability of a snowpack. The easiest method is to find a sample section of the slope where the immediate risk of danger from an

The potential for an avalanche cannot be determined simply by observing a snowy mountain.

avalanche is slight—either where the slope angle is shallow, near the bottom of the slope, or at the sides—and put weight on it. If the snow breaks away in slabs when a person walks or stomps on it, that is a sure sign of high avalanche danger.

A snowpack that holds a person's weight may or may not be stable. If the snowpack is under a great deal of stress, it may fracture as a person walks along it. Long, deep cracks indicate great instability.

Many avalanche experts listen for a particular sound as they test a snowfield. They generally describe it as a "whoompf" or "a belly-flop onto a feather mattress."[23] The sound indicates a collapsing layer of snow somewhere beneath the surface, and those who hear it are advised to leave the slope immediately.

On slopes where there is no safe section to test by walking, experts sometimes look for a cornice above the slope. Using a thin rope, they saw off a large section of the cornice and let it fall on the suspicious slope. If the snowpack is unstable, a falling cornice will usually trigger a snowslide.

Examining the Layers

The surest way of evaluating the stability of a snowpack is to examine each of its layers. Professionals use a number of methods to accomplish this, all of which involve digging with a shovel to expose a cross-section of the slope. Each layer of snow is then closely studied to see how the snow holds together in each layer, how well the layers have bonded with those above and below them, and how deep the snow is in each layer. In an effort to get a better feel for the overall condition of the pack, some professionals even use small paint brushes to dust away snow covering the layers or look through a strong magnifying glass to examine the shape of the crystals in the snow layers.

Although digging a snow pit is the most accurate method of predicting an avalanche, the method requires a basic understanding of snow crystals. Before using this method, experts urge that one enroll in a good class to learn exactly what to look for. Furthermore, digging snow pits is hard work and can be very time-consuming. This is especially true because the characteristics of a snowpack can change remarkably over a small area. The angle of the slope, and exposure to wind and sun, may be quite different within a short distance and may create different characteristics in the snowpack. The only way to be certain of the stability of the snow is to dig a new snow pit for each thousand-foot change of elevation, every significant change in orientation (the direction the slope faces), and for every new slope.

Unpredictability

Although experts have many tools for evaluating avalanche potential and can accurately identify areas of danger, an ele-

A man checks the composition of a snow pack, the best indicator of avalanche-prone snow.

The Rutschblock Test

There are many methods of probing a snowpack to test its stability. One of the most popular methods is the rutschblock test. This involves cutting out a block of snow as long as a pair of skies and at least six feet deep. What happens to that block when various degrees of stress are placed on it tells a great deal about the stability of the slope. For example, if the block shears and crumbles as it is being cut, the slope is extremely unstable and should be avoided at all costs. If the block falls apart when a person transfers weight onto it, it is slightly more stable but is still unsafe. If the block holds together while a skier jumps on top of it, the snowpack is very stable and should pose no avalanche danger. If a person can hop once on the snowpack before it begins to disintegrate, it is probably safe.

Quicker but less reliable methods include the shovel shear and the burp test. The shovel shear involves isolating a block of snow and pulling it forward with a shovel to see how easily the layers come loose. In a burp test, the snow block is tapped with a shovel to see if and where the snow layers break loose.

ment of unpredictability is involved with all avalanches. "With avalanches there is an element of luck,"[24] says avalanche control manager Alan Dennis. Snow crystals can change so quickly that a stable slope can become unstable overnight. Experts can often make good estimates of the potential size of an avalanche and the path that it is likely to take. Yet avalanches such as the one that struck Galtür, Austria, in 1999, occasionally defy the experts by bouncing at an odd angle off a canyon wall, by merging with other avalanches spawned at the same time, or by building up unexpectedly powerful airborne currents. Furthermore, the most experienced avalanche professional cannot predict when a slab will release, only the likelihood that it will.

A Close-Up View
of an Avalanche

An avalanche is a terrifying event. No other natural disaster strikes with the suddenness of snow crashing down a steep slope. One moment a mountainside can be a picture of beauty and peace as a soft snow blanket glistens silently under a brilliant winter sun. The next moment it can be a foaming, roaring, boiling mass of snow that annihilates everything in its path.

Every avalanche can be broken down into three main phases. The first phase is the fracture zone. This is the point at which the snowpack breaks away from the slope, thus beginning the avalanche. The higher up on a slope the fracture zone appears, the larger the avalanche is likely to be. The next phase is the gully or the chute. This is the path that the avalanche takes on its way down, where all of the actual dislocation of snow takes place. The final phase is the runout area. This is the flatter, more secure surface where the avalanche, with all its accumulated debris, grinds to a halt.

In the Fracture Zone

Since 95 percent of avalanche accidents are triggered by humans, there are countless stories from breathless and dazed survivors who were present the instant an avalanche started. No matter how much one prepares for or even anticipates the onslaught of an avalanche, the explosive collapse of a hillside into a runaway white tidal wave is stunning and unnerving. According to *The White Death* author McKay Jenkins, "If

there is anything typical about an avalanche, it is the total sur-
prise of the victim."[25]

Most of those survivors remember with crystal clarity the
sound that announced the triggering of the avalanche.
Depending on the pressures at work within the snowpack, the
ominous opening salvo can range greatly in tone and volume.
"Sometimes you hear a crack like thunder," says Sue Ferguson
of the U.S. Forest Service. "Sometimes the avalanche releases
quietly, like rustling silk."[26] A cold, densely packed slab is likely
to form hard crusts between layers that sound like a rifle shot
when a piece breaks away. In softer, deeper snow, the break

Survival Story #1: Double Whammy

Despite heavy snows, Franz Joseph set out from Stulen, Austria, on the morning of December 21, 1886, to deliver a load of flour. By midmorning the
snow was falling so thickly along the mountain road that he gave up and
turned back for home. Before long, he found his way blocked by an
avalanche that had fallen since he had passed that area. Franz Joseph set to
work with his shovel to clear a path to get himself back home.

He was still shoveling when a second avalanche struck. It carried Joseph
almost one thousand feet from the road before finally depositing him in a pile
of snow. Despite a broken leg, Joseph had nearly dug himself out of the shallow cover of snow when a third avalanche buried him under a mountain of
snow and debris. Unable to budge and encased in complete darkness, Joseph
eventually lost consciousness.

Fortunately for him, he had landed in a stream bed. It was warm enough
for the water to work its way through the heavy snowpack, thawing the solid
snow and creating large air spaces, which brought Joseph life-sustaining air.
The blessing nearly turned to a curse when the water became so deep that the
motionless Joseph nearly drowned.

After completely losing track of time, the trapped man felt a heavy sound-
ing rod strike him. He was able to move his hand enough to grab it and alert
those above to his presence. After surviving two avalanches in quick succession and twenty-nine hours in snowy captivity, Joseph was dug out and lived
to tell the tale.

Snow appears to have been poured down a slope in a soft-slab avalanche.

tends to be muffled. For Winston Cheyney, who triggered an avalanche in Colorado's Rocky Mountain National Park, it was the dreaded "whoompf" coming from deep under the snowpack as he advanced across it.

In all cases, the reaction of the snowpack to the trigger is likely to be rapid. Cheyney felt the snow beneath him settle back very quickly and then saw the entire surface of the slope shatter like a pane of glass, with the pieces all sliding down the slope. Hard-slab avalanches are likely to break into blocks as they begin their descent, while soft-slab avalanches tend to pour down a slope like sugar from a sack.

In the Chute

Once an avalanche starts, it may take one of several contrasting forms. Some avalanches flow slowly and ponderously like a river of cement. A wet-slab avalanche, for example, may slide downhill at a top speed of twenty miles per hour. More often, avalanches roar down the slope like a tidal wave. An average-size dry-slab avalanche will crash down a mountainside at speeds of sixty to eighty miles per hour. Sometimes, a very large avalanche will blast downhill like a white hurricane.

An avalanche may take several forms at once as it rages out of control. The avalanche that devastated Galtür swept down the mountainside in three waves: a top layer of swirling, powdery snow and air; a middle layer of denser, airborne snow; and a ground layer of the sliding snow mass.

The sound of the avalanche crescendos suddenly into what is described variously as hissing, rumbling surf or a speeding freight train. As the large blocks of a slab avalanche slide and roll downhill, they break up into smaller pieces. The descending snow triggers a chain reaction of slab fractures all the way

Like a white hurricane, an avalanche kicks up large clouds of snow.

down the hill, each of which adds more snow to the mass. The avalanche quickly and steadily grows larger and more powerful, becoming a torrent of snow that picks up rocks, tree branches, and other debris that lie in its path. A large avalanche may kick up a cloud of dust that rises hundreds of feet into the air.

All of this happens with stunning speed. A slab avalanche can accelerate many tons of snow to speeds approaching eighty miles per hour within five seconds of the initial trigger. As soon as Winston Cheyney realized he had triggered the avalanche that buried him in the Colorado Rockies, he started to run toward the side of the slope. But, as he remembers it, "I made it maybe one step or two before I felt the snow come up, kind of took my legs out from under me."[27] He estimated that the entire episode—from the initial crack to being buried under a mound of snow—could not have lasted more than a few seconds.

Peter Lew found himself in the chute of an avalanche while mountain climbing in Russia. Although he heard the avalanche coming from a great distance, he and his party were barely able to get clear of the path. "I really don't remember if it was the sound of the avalanche that warned us, but it must have been," he reported. "We had maybe 15 seconds from the time of the crevasse shift; we reacted in the last few seconds." Instinctively, Lew jumped into a crevasse and looked up as the avalanche passed. "I saw, distinctly, a solid wall of snow shooting out, going incredibly fast, blocking out the sky in the darkness and roar."[28]

Shawn Marcus narrowly avoided being swept away in an avalanche at the Holt Creek Drainage in British Columbia, Canada, on March 25, 2001. Even though the snow never touched him, he was knocked off his feet by the blast of wind that preceded the snow. "It was the strongest wind I've ever felt,"[29] he said.

Thrown into a Waterfall

The sensation of being in the chute of an avalanche is something like experiencing an incredibly large earthquake with the ground tilted at a steep angle. Some people have described it as being thrown into the center of a large waterfall. Ground that was solid only a moment ago suddenly turns into a substance that acts very much like a liquid. Cheyney was in midstep when the sliding snow took his legs out from under him. No sooner had he fallen on his back than the avalanche launched him into the air. He flew helplessly for hundreds of feet before he landed in a deep pile of snow.

Survival Story #2

Mining companies sometimes go to great lengths to dig valuable minerals such as gold out of remote mountains. When one of the richest gold deposits in the world was discovered in the Coast Mountains of British Columbia, investors poured $55 million into a mining operation in 1964. The camp at the Leduc Glacier was still being constructed in February 1965 when a series of incredible snowstorms hit the area. Over sixteen feet of snow fell within a single week.

Oblivious to the dangers of heavy snow in the mountains, mining operators sent in extra workers to keep the area clear so progress on the camps could continue. Meanwhile, the snows had created enormous snow bombs on the slopes high above the camp, just waiting for the slightest pressure to set off the explosion.

On February 18 disaster struck. Millions of tons of snow broke loose, so silently that the survivors claimed that it had come on them without any warning. Eino Myllyla, a carpenter, was one of those buried in the mountain of snow. Over the next three days he lost and regained consciousness, unaware that huge rescue helicopters were landing and taking off from the surface directly above him.

With twenty-six men known dead, rescue workers had long given up on finding any more survivors when a bulldozer clearing the site exposed some of the carpenter's clothing. After seventy-nine hours trapped in the snow, Myllyla was pulled out and flown to a hospital. Although hospitalized for several months from the effects of frostbite, hypothermia, and oxygen depletion, thirty-two-year-old Myllyla somehow survived.

Recognizing the futility of trying to protect such a location from avalanches, the mining operation closed, never to reopen.

Survivors of an avalanche often describe the sensation of being pulled into a giant waterfall.

The greatest dangers to a person caught in the chute phase of an avalanche are broken bones from being twisted into awkward positions as they are swept downhill, being dashed against solid objects such as trees or rocks or struck by debris within the avalanche such as tree limbs, rocks, skis, or snowmobiles. Matthias Zdarsky, a young Austrian soldier who spent considerable time stationed in the Alps during World War I, provided one of the most vivid examples of the damage that a large avalanche can inflict in midrun. Although he survived a terrifying scare in an avalanche in 1916, Zdarsky was so brutally smashed, crunched, and twisted on his downhill ride that he suffered a total of eighty fractures and dislocations.

The Runout

The runout zone can be even more deadly than the chute. Although some avalanches, particularly smaller ones, gradually disperse or grind to a halt, many of them slam into the runout zone at the peak of their fury. The power of an avalanche, whether in the form of powdered airborne snow or a solid, tumbling wall of snow, can be almost unimaginable. In 1920 six forestry workers in Glarus, Switzerland, were smashed to death by a wave of airborne powder created by a large slab avalanche. A seventh worker survived a harrowing ride in which he was sucked up an estimated twenty-two hundred feet in the air and carried a mile and a half across the valley, where he had the good fortune to land in a cushioning pile of soft snow.

The incredible wind speeds turn snowflakes into millions of tiny bullets that batter everything in their path. The clutter of debris scoured from the slopes and torn out of the forests provides the avalanche with deadly missiles of a different sort.

The enormous pressure differences caused by the dry-powder wind speeds can blow out windows, destroy a wooden-frame house, knock down trees, and even pull people out of their homes. At about the same time that Galtür was devastated by avalanches in February 1999, another one ravaged a popular ski resort in nearby Chamonix, France. An American visitor commented, "I've seen many avalanches, but not the type that come into your house and blow it away. It was more like a California earthquake."[30]

Moving Mountains of Snow

The moving mountain of snow that follows an airborne blast strikes with a different kind of irresistible force. Japanese researchers have measured the impact of a large avalanche at 160 tons per square yard. This is almost fifty times the force

Rescuers in Chamonix, France, stand amid the wreckage of an avalanche that destroyed several chalets.

needed to utterly destroy a wooden-frame house. Survivors of an avalanche in the Alps in 1999 witnessed this power from close range. "The chalet next to ours disappeared—it was pushed across the road," said one witness. "There were blocks of cement and gravel everywhere. It was the apocalypse!"[31]

John Tweedy, an avalanche controller who works in some of the world's most active avalanche country in British Columbia, finds such statements all too believable. "More than once we've [had] meter-high [3-foot-high] concrete guard rails, in three-meter [10-foot] sections locked together, blown off the road."[32] Other witnesses have reported seeing a large section of an iron bridge tossed 150 feet in the air.

Large snowslides have been known to crush concrete buildings. Although thick stands of trees are generally considered to be good protection against avalanches, occasionally an avalanche will grow to such an enormous size that it destroys an entire forest. In 1968 thirteen people were killed and twenty chalets destroyed in an area of the Swiss Alps that was widely considered to be safe from avalanches because a dense pine forest protected the village. In this case, the sheer size of the avalanche overwhelmed everything in its path.

The most powerful avalanche ever encountered in the United States occurred in 1982 at the California ski resort of Alpine Meadows, near Lake Tahoe. Following record snowfall, a slab ten feet deep and three thousand feet wide broke loose on the high slopes. With the deep snow of the lower hills providing more fuel for the disaster, the avalanche grew to thirty feet high within a matter of seconds. More than sixty-five thousand tons of snow slammed into the resort at the runout zone at a speed of eighty miles per hour, killing seven people and causing $2 million in damage.

"Ten Thousand Wild Beasts"

The most devastating avalanche ever recorded took place on January 10, 1962, in the Andes Mountains of Peru, where its victims were mountain villagers. During the late afternoon, a warm sun beat down on the northwest slope of the 22,205-foot

The awesome might of an avalanche leaves little untouched in its path.

Nevado Huascaran, the tallest peak in the country. At 6:13 P.M., a large slab of snow broke loose and fell more than half a mile onto an enormous snowfield that scientists had labeled Glacier 511. The jolt sent some 3 million tons of ice plummeting down the steep slopes. With a crashing sound that one witness likened to "like that of ten thousand wild beasts,"[33] the huge mass bounced off canyon walls, shearing loose tons of rocks.

The avalanche grew into a swirling, foaming mass of snow, ice, and debris at least 1.5 miles wide and 175 feet thick. It roared downhill with such force that it lifted boulders weighing thousands of tons onto ledges and ridges more than 200 feet above the canyon. On its journey down the mountain, it flattened and buried everything in its path. The small village of Yanamachico was erased from the face of the earth—only eight of the village's eight hundred inhabitants survived. Farther downhill, the much larger town of Ranrahirca lay buried under a sea of frozen mud, with an official estimate of at least twenty-seven hundred dead.

By the time it had finished its nine-mile descent, the avalanche had destroyed six villages and had severely damaged

Villagers in Ranrahirca, Peru, stand atop frozen, mud-covered homes demolished by an avalanche in 1962.

three others, killing an estimated four thousand people and ten thousand animals. When it finally came to a halt, it completely blocked the Santa River, eventually causing a flood that swept away all of the downstream bridges and carried bodies a hundred miles out to sea.

The Huascaran avalanche was certainly atypical. Nonetheless, it provided a horrific reminder of the potential power of an avalanche.

Buried Alive

Although the force of an avalanche can cause massive destruction, the vast majority of avalanche deaths occur through suffocation. Whether the victims are caught in the fracture zone and are swept along down the chute or are at the bottom of the hill in the runout zone, their fate is generally the same. As the avalanche reaches the runout zone, the snow piles to enormous depths. Unless the victim is lucky enough to have landed near the top of the snow heap, he or she is buried under several feet of snow.

In the final seconds before the avalanche grinds to a complete halt, the snow undergoes a change that is terrifying to

Survival Story #3: Ski Resort Disaster

Following record snowfalls in late March 1982, the slopes surrounding Alpine Meadows ski resort in California were ripe for avalanches. Worse yet, a blizzard continued to dump snow at the rate of two to three feet per day. Vicious winds with gusts of up to 125 miles per hour further packed snow into mountainous drifts. The resort's avalanche control team worked furiously to clear the slopes. But after four days of battling the elements, they realized they were fighting a losing battle and closed the slopes to skiing.

The next day, as conditions continued to worsen, most of the resort's employees were sent home as a safety precaution. On the afternoon of March 30, the few remaining employees heard a low whistle that changed almost instantly to a sound like a howling wind. The shock waves hit first, followed by an unearthly roaring as blasts of wind swept down the slope. Buildings exploded and steel beams were bent and twisted. Every structure on the resort, covering an area of five acres, was obliterated.

Anna Conrad, a ski-lift operator could do nothing but crouch in terror as the building around her blew apart. Within moments, tons of snow poured down on her, leaving her dazed and disoriented. "It was black," she told David Cupp in his *National Geographic* article "Winter's White Death." "I had no idea where I was or what had happened."

It turned out that she was luckier than seven of her coworkers, who died in the avalanche. Just before the wave of snow buried her, rows of lockers fell across a bench next to her, providing her with a five-foot-long, two-foot-high air space. Once she realized her situation, Conrad was able to pull clothes out of the lockers to keep herself warm.

Rescuers had no idea where anyone was in the twenty-foot-deep mountain of snow that covered the resort. Conrad huddled for two days without any sign of help. On April 2 a German shepherd named Bridget picked up her scent and led rescuers near where she was buried ten feet beneath them. But the continuing snowstorm brought a renewed avalanche danger, and the crews were forced to abandon their digging.

The crew did not return until April 5, and began shoveling snow where the dog had indicated. By this time, they were certain they were doing nothing more than recovering bodies. Conrad, however, had managed to survive for five days by eating snow. Rescue workers were stunned when they found her alive amid the lockers. Although she lost her right foot and much of her left foot to frostbite, Conrad had lived through the worst ski resort disaster in U.S. history.

Rescuers desperately search for victims in the aftermath of the 1962 Ranrahirca avalanche.

those caught in it. During the early part of the avalanche, the snow is very fluid—almost like the air in a blizzard. Movement of arms and legs is unrestricted, although those caught in the avalanche are usually tumbling so wildly that they cannot coordinate their movements. Then, in just a few seconds, the avalanche comes to a halt, and the snow packs so densely that most who have survived the experience describe a feeling of being encased in cement. A person trapped under even a foot or two of snow is helpless. Cut off from the light, he or she is unable to see and is often unable to move any muscle even a fraction of an inch.

The sudden change—from an eerie floating sensation as the victims hurtle downward to complete paralysis when the flow stops—is completely disorienting. The victims are usually so confused that they have no idea which way is up. Most survivors of this situation recall a feeling of panic. Unable to cope with the situation, the brain eventually becomes numb and the victims lose consciousness. Their only hope for survival is that someone on top of the snow will find them and dig them out.

Survival and Rescue

Although luck plays a role in surviving an avalanche, people who go out into the winter mountains prepared for trouble have a much better chance of coming home alive than those who ignore safety precautions. At a minimum, venturing into avalanche territory alone or in mediocre health is inviting trouble.

Experts advise that members of an outdoor recreation party keep a comfortable distance from each other in potential avalanche terrain. They caution against the mountain climbers' practice of roping people together. Not only can it drag a person who would otherwise be safe into an avalanche, but injuries can also occur when people are caught up in a rope during the violent fall.

Savvy climbers will, whenever possible, climb or descend a questionable slope on the edges, and cross either above or below the slope. "If forced to negotiate dangerous areas," writes Robert Young Pelton in *Come Back Alive*, "climb or cross them one person at a time. That way, if misfortune strikes, there will be someone to dig you out."[34] Experts advise those crossing a questionable slope to move quickly and, wherever possible, to take temporary refuge in stands of trees or large outcroppings. It is important to plan ahead and have an escape route picked out should something trigger an avalanche.

Survival Equipment

Basic avalanche survival gear includes probes, radio beacons, and shovels. None of these items are of any use during an

Experts advise recreationists to pack basic survival gear such as probes, radio beacons, and shovels.

avalanche; all serve the most important function of avalanche rescue, which is to quickly locate and uncover victims buried in the snow. Probes have been used for centuries in avalanches to locate buried persons. The modern version is a lightweight collapsible pole, similar to a tent pole, that can be extended to a length of twelve feet. Poles work well because they can break through hard-packed snow.

Battery-operated radio beacons have become the quickest and most effective means of locating a person buried in an avalanche. These small devices, which are worn under clothing, send out a constant electromagnetic impulse that can be picked up by other transceivers in the area. They are effective only if the batteries are fresh (rechargeable batteries are not recommended), every member of the group carries one, and everyone remembers to travel with the transmission switch on. If anyone in the group disappears under an avalanche, the others can locate the signal of the missing person by turning their sets to receive.

Neither probes nor beacons are of any use without a shovel to dig out the victims. Although lightweight plastic shovels are available, they are not always large enough. Avalanche victims may be trapped under many feet of tightly packed snow and require a sizable shovel blade to do the job.

Other avalanche equipment includes medical kits to treat the injured and flares to alert rescue crews of the location. Releasable bindings are an important safety feature for

New Technology

In recent years researchers have tried a number of technological innovations to increase the chances of surviving an avalanche. Radio beacons have been the most effective innovation in avalanche safety. But two experimental products that recently hit the market show potential.

One of these is the Avalung. This is a device that acts as a filter to pull air from the snowpack. It also vents carbon dioxide to prevent it from freezing and forming the dreaded ice mask that forms an impenetrable barrier around avalanche victims, even in porous snow. The main drawback is that a person needs almost immediate access to the Avalung at the onset of the avalanche in order for it to work.

A second innovation is the airbag, which has been tested primarily in the Alps. The airbag is worn in a backpack. When an avalanche occurs, the person pulls a cord that inflates the bag with air or helium. This keeps the person afloat on top of the avalanche and may protect them from trauma or from being buried in deep snow. In the winter of 2000, avalanche airbags were activated thirty-six times. In only one case was there a fatality—a strong indication that the airbags are lifesaving devices.

backcountry skiers to prevent skis from causing injury in an avalanche. Some outdoor recreationists also carry a magnifying glass for inspecting the snowpack layers, a snow saw, and even a magnometer for detecting metal beneath the snow.

One piece of equipment that is not recommended is an avalanche cord. This is a long, slender, brightly colored rope with one end attached to a person's waist and the other left trailing. The idea behind using the rope is the hope that part of it may end up on top of the snow and lead rescuers to the buried person attached to it. However, following such a cord requires digging a deep trench in hopes of finding a person who may be quite a distance away. This can be extremely time-consuming, and time is of the essence in recovering any person missing in an avalanche.

Experts say the best protection against avalanches is to always carry the proper rescue equipment and then to make decisions as if you do not have it. Many a winter recreationist has gotten into difficulty by relying too heavily on technology and forgetting to show the proper respect for the power of nature.

Releasable bindings on snow skis may help prevent severe injury in an avalanche.

When an Avalanche Strikes

Since avalanches can accelerate to speeds of eighty miles per hour in a matter of seconds, there is no use trying to outrun one. The hiker's or climber's only chance of escaping an approaching avalanche is to get to the side of the slope immediately. For those caught on skis or a snowboard, the best advice is to go straight down to build up speed and then head for the side. According to skier Dolores LaChapelle, "When an avalanche begins, if you slam your skis down hard you can often ski out of it."[35]

Snowmobiles are powerful and fast enough to offer some hope of escape. If a snowmobile is going uphill when the avalanche is triggered, experts advise continuing to accelerate up the hill in hopes of riding over it. If crossing a hill, the best procedure is to continue at top speed.

When escape is impossible, the first survival technique is to get rid of all encumbering equipment. Nearly a third of avalanche deaths are due to trauma, so it is important to get away from objects that could cause injury in the swirling chaos, such as snowmobiles, skis, poles, and backpacks.

Mountain climbers can sometimes dig in deep with their ice picks or axes to anchor themselves while the snow slides past them, but this works only in shallow snow or surface avalanches. Occasionally, natural handholds may be available. Mountaineer Yvon Chouinard notes, "It may be that the best reason for staying in the trees is you can grab one on the way down."[36] Chouinard goes on to point out, however, that this should be attempted only at the very start of the incident, before picking up speed. Trees, boulders, and bushes can be false security. They are likely to cause more harm than good to a person hurtling out of control downhill.

Staying Alive in the Slide

Anyone caught in a large avalanche is almost completely helpless for the duration of the slide. Nonetheless, some actions can sometimes increase survival chances. On the most basic level, persons caught in an avalanche can use their arms to protect their heads against injury from striking or being struck by objects.

Since an avalanche acts as a liquid during the slide, using a swimming motion may be helpful. Some experts recommend trying to stay on top of the surf by using an action like treading water. Others suggest the backstroke because a person who is buried face up in an avalanche has almost double the odds of survival as someone buried face down. Victims who manage to keep their bearings are sometimes able to swim toward the side of the avalanche. In the middle of an avalanche, however, it is often difficult to know which way is up, much less find the side of the slope.

Although the natural inclination for someone on the verge of being buried under tons of snow is to gulp air as fast and furiously as possible, this can be fatal. Avalanche victims have been found suffocated because their wide-open mouths were stuffed with compacted snow that prevented them from exhaling.

The Crucial Time

Many experts, including Pelton, advise "keeping your greatest efforts for when you feel the avalanche slow down, because as it slows, powder snow compresses. This is the critical point at which your survival is determined."[37]

These few moments are crucial because they are a person's last chance to help himself or herself. If the victims can get the smallest part of their bodies above the snow surface, they stand a good chance of being rescued. Over three-fourths of those with a protruding body part are pulled out of avalanches alive, and many of the remaining one-quarter die only because no one was in the area to find them.

If getting to the surface is not possible, the alternative is making a last-ditch effort, using arms, legs, and body, to create an air space. The amount of air space determines how long a person will last buried under the snow. All snow contains some air space. "The good news is that even dense avalanche debris is 60 to 70 percent air and you can breath that air, at

Survival sometimes depends on finding an air space under a mound of snow.

least for a few minutes,"[38] observes Bruce Tremper. That is why 93 percent of those who survive an avalanche slide remain alive for at least fifteen minutes. After that time, however, the air runs out quickly.

Virtually everyone who has survived a prolonged period under snow has done so because some sort of air space was present. Three women in Bergemoletto, Italy, survived for thirty-seven days under an avalanche because they had the good fortune to be buried in a livestock stable that did not collapse. Not only did the they have plenty of air, but they also had goats that provided the milk that kept them alive.

Most avalanche victims are not that lucky, however. Their lives may depend on their ability to create a small wedge of air space. They can do this by throwing up an arm or hand in front of their faces during the moments when the avalanche settles. Even a quick movement of the head may create an air pocket that could provide life-saving minutes for a person lying face up. The small air pocket that may form when a face-down person is pressed into the snow does no good, however, since the mouth and nose will be pushed into the snow by the weight of the head.

Once the snow has settled, a person can do little to increase his or her survival chances. Most victims cannot move at all, much less dig themselves out. Those covered shallowly might be able to work a finger up to the surface, if they know which direction is up. A trapped person can sometimes determine direction by forcing saliva out of their mouth. Whichever way gravity pulls the saliva is down.

The one thing that a trapped person can do is call for help. "Dozens of shallowly buried avalanche victims have been recovered alive when rescuers heard yells come from under the snow,"[39] according to avalanche expert Dale Atkins. Other than that, the best advice is to avoid struggling and remain as calm as possible to conserve oxygen. Although the situation is terrifying, it is not hopeless. The vast majority of those buried in avalanches are dug out alive.

Companion Rescue

Time and snow depth are the key factors in determining the success of an avalanche rescue. The survival rate for people buried in an avalanche plunges rapidly from over 90 percent in the first fifteen minutes to 30 percent after thirty-five minutes. Only 3 percent of those extracted after spending two hours in the snow come out alive. Because time is so crucial, in most cases there is no time to call in a professional rescue team. More than two-thirds of those who survive being buried by an avalanche are rescued by members of their own party. In fact, John Hart advises in *Walking Softly in the Wilderness*, "It is almost never worth the loss of time"[40] to send for help. Others advocate spending an hour searching before getting help unless the slope conditions are too dangerous or help is very near.

According to Atkins, the first rule of any search and rescue is "don't create a bigger incident than what already exists."[41] Avalanches occur on unstable slopes, which means that where there is one avalanche, there may well be others. Many of the most devastating avalanches have been followed almost imme-

The Perils of Traveling Alone

Although some outdoor enthusiasts revel in the silence and solitude of nature, traveling alone in avalanche country is asking for trouble, even for an expert. At 8:30 A.M. on April 3, 2001, Chad Jones took off on his snowmobile into the mountains of Summit County, Colorado. An experienced guide for a local snowmobile outfit, Jones wanted to explore an area of national forest that the company had not previously used and possibly establish a new trail there.

Jones's machine apparently got stuck at the bottom of a gully. While he was trying to work himself free, a small soft-slab avalanche buried him under four to five feet of snow.

Several hours later friends became concerned when he had not returned and set out to look for him. They followed his tracks to the avalanche, where they found a part of the snowmobile sticking up through the snow. They immediately began probing uphill, but by the time they found Jones, he was dead.

The small size of the avalanche, which slid less than 75 yards downhill over a width of between 80 and 180 feet, made the incident especially tragic. Jan Reuter, writing for the *Summit County Daily News*, quoted national forest law enforcement officer Tom Healy as saying, "If someone had been riding with him, it's possible they would have seen it happen and been able to rescue him."

diately by other avalanches in the same area. In 1958 a rescue team in Utah was allowed to scatter along an unstable slope in search of avalanche victims. This compounded the original disaster when one of the rescuers fell victim to a second avalanche.

In all cases, the most important thing a companion can do to rescue someone caught in an avalanche is to carefully note the place where the victim or victims were last seen. The history of avalanche disasters are filled with stories of precious search time lost because witnesses gave mistaken, confusing, or conflicting information about the avalanche scene.

The search starts at the point where the victim was last seen and continues downhill, following the course of the avalanche down to the runout zone. Rescuers then quickly look over the area for clues about the missing person's whereabouts, a procedure known as the hasty search. This search will uncover obvious signs, such as a hand sticking up or a piece of clothing, or less obvious signs, such as a ski pole or an item from a backpack that could give a general idea of the location. Searchers also listen carefully for a muffled voice from beneath the snow.

According to Atkins, poorly conducted hasty searches are one of the most common and heartbreaking mistakes in avalanche rescue. One of the most tragic examples occurred in December 1984 near Aspen, Colorado. Two backcountry skiers were swept down a mountain by a slide. One of the skiers managed to dig himself out. But after quickly checking for signs of his friend and finding nothing, he left the site to get help. Hours later, a rescue team found a ski tip poking up out of the snow. In shallow snow beneath the ski was the body of the second skier. Had the clue been spotted immediately, the man would likely have survived.

Finding Buried Victims

If members of the party are wearing transceivers, the rescuers immediately switch theirs to the receive position. Transceivers, however, are not foolproof indicators of where someone is buried. Some knowledge of how to conduct a transceiver recovery is necessary, as victims of an avalanche in Colorado in 1988 nearly found out to their misfortune. Three of the four skiers in a well-equipped group of skiers were engulfed in an avalanche. All were wearing transceivers, but the one who had avoided the avalanche had no training in how to use the beacons. Fortunately for them all, this skier located one of the others and dug him out in time. The rescued skier was experienced with the use of the radio beacons and used his transceiver to find and rescue the others.

To begin a beacon search, the rescuer must get close enough to pick up the beacon signal. Then, by tracing a gridlike pattern and noting where the signal appears and where it does not, the location is narrowed to six feet. At this point, rescuers decide exactly where to dig by holding the beacon close to the snow and pinpointing the location of the strongest signal.

If no clues, either visual or electromagnetic, are present, searchers must then begin probing with their poles. A coarse probe consists of searchers walking elbow to elbow, probing the snow every few feet with their poles, starting from the runout zone and working their way up. If they hit an object under the snow, they begin shoveling. If enough rescuers are available, a shovel crew will do the digging while the probers keep going in case it turns out to be a false lead. If the coarse probe fails, searchers close ranks and go over the ground again in a fine probe, during which they jab poles into the snow at much closer intervals. Once one person is located and uncovered, the searchers move on to locate any others who are missing before spending time treating the injured.

Coarse probes are usually successful; 7 out of 10 persons buried in less than 10 feet of snow are found by this method. But because of the time required to conduct the search, even this method is far more likely to find a dead body than a living person. "Once probe lines begin," warns Atkins, "the speed of

Rescuers search for survivors after an avalanche in Ticino, Switzerland in February 2001.

Hopes run high as a search party digs through snow that buried two snow boarders in Neidernsill, Austria in 2000.

any rescue falls dramatically."[42] Of 140 individuals located by probes on U.S. slopes between 1951 and 1998, 121 were already dead.

A person's chances of surviving an avalanche drop significantly when he or she is buried at a depth of more than four feet. In the United States only one person has survived who was buried in seven feet or more of snow.

The deeper the snow, the harder it is to locate the person. In snow deeper than the twelve-foot length of the standard probe, trenches often have to be dug. Once searchers have to resort to trenches and fine probes, they concede that they are no longer involved in rescue but rather in recovery of a body.

Nonetheless, a few remarkable people have beaten the odds both in depth of snow and length of interment. A Swiss mountain guide was once dug out alive after being buried in twenty-two feet of snow for four hours. Because of such cases, rescuers are urged to continue their search for six to eight hours before giving up hope.

Rescue Teams

In highly populated winter mountain locations such as ski resorts, trained avalanche rescue teams are often on duty. They are able to move quickly into any terrain by hiking, climbing, skiing, snowmobiling, and even using helicopters in some cases. The job can be dangerous as it may summon rescuers onto dangerous slopes. Yet avalanche professionals understand the nature of avalanches so well that, despite the danger they often face, they make up less than 0.5 percent of avalanche fatalities.

Increasingly, the experts have been turning to dogs to take on the task of finding avalanche victims. Each human body continually gives off a characteristic odor that is able to percolate through nearly a dozen feet of snow. A dog, whose sense of smell is ten thousand times more sensitive than a human's, is adept at detecting that scent. When the wind is right, some dogs can pick it up at a distance of two hundred yards and quickly trace it to its source. Atkins notes, "The nose of a trained avalanche dog is perhaps the most efficient search tool a rescuer has."[43] A team of twenty human rescue workers would need four hours to thoroughly search a snow mass the size of a football field. A single trained dog can

A trained avalanche dog can detect the scent of a human two hundred yards away or trapped in twelve feet of snow.

cover the same ground in about twenty-five minutes, and do so more safely.

Trainers such as Deb Franson, who works in the Teton Mountains of Wyoming, train dogs by giving them a series of gradually more difficult tasks. They begin by playing a game in which they must find their trainer, who is within sight. Next, the trainer hides and the dogs try to find him or her. Finally, the dogs are asked to find a volunteer buried in the snow. Advanced avalanche dog training exercises include asking a dog to find three or four people under six feet of snow while being bombarded by artificial distractions.

Some dogs show a remarkable skill at these exercises and have found people hidden under nearly twenty feet of snow. "I've seen Kiva [a trained dog] find someone in a drill in less than three minutes," says Jack Eckland of Modesto, California, who learned firsthand the effectiveness of avalanche dogs. While working at the Kirkwood Ski Resort in California in 1993, Eckland was caught in a large avalanche. The rolling snowpack smashed Eckland into a tree, which broke his back and several ribs and then encased him under five feet of snow. "I was folded up backwards by that slide and couldn't move a finger,"[44] says Eckland.

An avalanche dog named Doc was soon on the scene. Almost at once, Doc trotted over to the clump of trees and started digging. "I was buried way down there against a tree and close to passing out when I felt his paw hit my back," says Eckland. "I owe my life to that dog. Without him it would have been several hours before they found me."[45] In Wyoming that same year a dog recovered a live victim buried in over six feet of snow.

Avalanche dogs, however, do not guarantee a successful search. Contamination of the slope by other searchers, whose smells mingle with those of the victims, can make a dog's task nearly impossible. Wet, dense, and extremely deep snow; strong winds; blizzards; and rain can also severely hamper a dog's effectiveness. Furthermore, a great deal of time and expense is involved in training dogs, and only some of the larger resort areas have the resources to maintain them.

Rescue Dogs

Dogs have been used in winter mountain rescue operations for more than three hundred years. This unique service began by accident when residents of St. Bernard's Hospice in the Swiss Alps brought in and bred enormous dogs to serve as guard dogs. Over the years the dogs, which became known as St. Bernards, showed a remarkable skill at finding their way in terrible blizzard conditions. The hospice began training them to assist travelers, who commonly ran into trouble in the unpredictable weather around St. Bernard Pass.

One St. Bernard dog in particular became famous in the nineteenth century. Barry I was said to have saved more than forty lives, including that of a child whom he licked to consciousness and dragged back to safety. Contrary to the popular legend that arose, however, neither Barry nor the other St. Bernards ever carried alcoholic beverages in containers around their necks.

The use of dogs as avalanche rescuers also came about by accident. In 1937 a member of a Swiss rescue team took his dog Moritzli along to an avalanche site. The team uncovered all but one of the victims and was looking for the last when Moritzli kept returning to the same spot in the snow and barking. The team finally took their cue and began digging at the spot. They uncovered a live victim who most likely would have died had the dog not located him. The incident prompted avalanche experts to begin training dogs as part of their rescue teams.

Today many winter recreation areas employ dogs as an important part of their rescue teams. Experts say that no one breed works better than any other. They find more differences in ability between dogs of the same breed than between dogs of different breeds. Since all dogs have keen senses of smell, the most important characteristics for an avalanche rescue dog are the desire to please, the ability to move through snow, and the ability to handle stress.

As with all rescue attempts, the greatest challenge is locating a person in time. Survival time is so limited for buried persons that, in the vast majority of cases, a buried victim is already dead by the time the dogs arrive. The sudden onset of avalanches means that most rescue attempts will continue to depend on those already on the scene at the time of the incidents.

Living with Avalanches

A valanches are a fact of life. Given the realities of snowfall and slope angles in the mountains, there is no way to prevent them from occurring. Nonetheless, major avalanche catastrophes provoke outrage among the public, who demand that the government and private enterprises take steps to protect them. These demands are somewhat unrealistic, however, since the vast majority of avalanche fatalities in the United States and Canada take place in the backcountry, far from population centers or transportation routes, where no avalanche control is available.

Public officials and resort owners in many mountainous regions have gone to great lengths to minimize the damage that these inevitable snowslides can cause. Austria, a mountainous country in the Alps, has spent more than $700 million since 1945 on avalanche disaster prevention.

Three basic strategies are used to protect the public from sliding snow: active defusing of dangerous slopes, passive protection measures, and education.

Explosives

When avalanche professionals talk about bombing the slopes, they are not talking about racing downhill on skis. Rather, they are referring to the practice of lobbing explosives onto mountain slopes to trigger avalanches.

This practice is the most effective means of defusing potentially dangerous avalanche conditions. The principle is simple. Rather than allowing the slopes to build up massive amounts of unstable snow that could result in a catastrophic avalanche, controllers use explosives to trigger smaller avalanches that rid the slopes of the snow. These small avalanches are set off at times when the areas are cleared of people, usually in the early morning.

The use of explosives in avalanche control dates back to Switzerland some time after World War I. It was not until a few decades later, however, that the practice became standard procedure in many mountain areas. During World War II, the United States trained a special group of soldiers, the Tenth Mountain Division, to cope with the mountain conditions they would encounter while fighting in the Alps. When they returned home following the war, some of them put their experience to use in the developing ski areas in the western United States. One of these was Monty Atwater, who, in 1948, began experimenting with explosives to clear dangerous slopes.

Controlled explosives clear snow on dangerous slopes, thereby reducing avalanche danger.

An Avalanche as a Weapon of Mass Destruction

The first use of explosives to trigger avalanches had nothing to do with avalanche control. In December 1916, during World War I, Italian and Austrian troops were engaged in bitter fighting in the Dolomite Mountains when a snowstorm struck. The two armies hunkered down as three days of heavy snow were followed by gale-force winds that packed the snow into towering drifts.

When the weather cleared, the forces resumed the fight. As they lobbed artillery shells at their foes, a sinister side effect became apparent. David Cupp, writing for *National Geographic*, quotes Austrian soldier Erwin Aichinger as saying, "Both sides noticed that their shell fire triggered avalanches. A dreadful idea took hold. Gunners raised their sights to the mountain tops, where great snow masses hung, and sent them crashing down."

Estimates of the resulting carnage vary. But even low-end estimates set the figure at about eighteen thousand deaths.

Some of the compounds he used were so powerful that they nearly killed him, but in the process he discovered that the shock vibrations were more important than the size of the blast in producing the desired results.

For a number of years avalanche removal with explosives was a hazardous job. Experts like Atwater used wire fuses that required them to go out onto the dangerous slopes to plant their explosives. During the mid-1950s ignition caps and fuses made the job easier. After experimentation showed that the vibrations that trigger avalanches travel more efficiently in the air, safety experts began stringing the explosives along wires above the snow-packed slopes.

Sometimes avalanche clearers would use military howitzers to launch explosives onto more remote or dangerous slopes. This was relatively inefficient and costly until the 1950s, when the recoilless rifle was developed. Later modified to a form known as the avalauncher, which is still in use today, the device consisted of a long barrel attached to a cylinder of compressed air. The device was nicknamed "the soup gun" because researchers in the early 1960s used cans of soup, which were the same size and shape as the explosive charge used with the guns, as ammunition in tests. Since then, avalanche controllers have launched hundreds of thousands of canisters of explosives on U.S. and Canadian slopes.

Modern Avalanche Triggering

The typical explosive used today is either a gel dynamite or ammonium nitrate. Virtually every major U.S. winter recreation area now employs experts to clear the slopes of dangerously heavy snows. In ski resort areas, the experts typically do their work in the early morning darkness, before the skiers get out onto the hills.

Avalanche triggering is also common in areas where potential avalanche hazards threaten major transportation routes. One of the most heavily traveled highways in avalanche country is the Snoqualmie Pass outside of Seattle, Washington. With an annual snowfall that averages over four hundred inches in some areas, this pass is often piled with wet, heavy,

Avalanche triggering is used in areas where roads need to remain clear for travel.

dangerous snows. But because so many people use the road, officials constantly bombard the slopes with explosives to keep the area safe for travelers.

Aggressive avalanche control through explosives has proved remarkably successful in the United States. Colorado, which has the most heavily traveled mountain roads in the nation, has not recorded a driver fatality in nearly forty years.

The method is not, however, as widely used in other countries. Alpine mountains are generally higher, steeper, and more populated than North American mountains. Triggering avalanches under such conditions may do more harm than good. According to Dale Atkins, "In Europe they don't use explosives to trigger avalanches because they don't know how big the avalanches will be when they release them."[46]

Furthermore, avalanche conditions are so common in many parts of the Alps that a costly and irritating constant bombardment would be necessary to attempt to control each one. In January 1981 some valleys in Switzerland averaged more than four avalanches per square mile.

Even in the United States avalanche explosives have introduced a new and disturbing danger. Experts estimate that 5 percent of the explosives fail to explode when launched. That means that thousands of unexploded rounds are scattered around U.S. mountain recreation areas. Some of these are likely to explode spontaneously. The more explosive shells lobbed into the mountains, the greater the risk of injuries from these hidden dangers.

Passive Protection

The most common alternative to the use of explosives has been limiting the destructive effects of avalanches through passive protection in the form of either natural or artificial barriers. Thick forests offer some of the best protection against avalanches. They stabilize slopes by anchoring snowpacks, blocking the wind to prevent massive drifting of snow, and by forming barriers to stop, slow down, or diffuse the sliding snow.

Unfortunately, in many avalanche areas people have cleared forests to provide heating fuel, construction materials for development, and open slopes for skiers.

Woodcutters in the Alps cleared many mountain forests hundreds of years ago, and some of the great avalanche disasters in western North America in the nineteenth century roared through areas where forests had been recently cut down. In ski resort areas throughout the world, slopes have been cleared of trees to create ski runs, greatly increasing snowpack instability.

All of this has taken place despite the long-recognized value of forests in avalanche control. As early as 1397 the Swiss village of Andermatt passed a law protecting the remaining vegetation after the surrounding forests nearly disappeared. The village is still protected today by a triangular stand of trees on the slope just above it. Many villages in the Alps, however, did little or nothing to lessen the damage done to the forests hundreds of years ago, and now it is too late.

Modern engineers have developed artificial barriers in an effort to control avalanches. Following a series of avalanche disasters in 1951 that created public outrage, Switzerland began building steel and stone fences on the mountainsides to protect the villages below. More than 250 miles of such structures now line the nation's slopes. Steel snow fences have also been constructed to provide stability for snow on the slopes.

But engineers acknowledge that the largest avalanches simply sweep over and through such barriers. As a result, they have concentrated their efforts on steering avalanche paths around humans rather than trying to stop them altogether. Many Alpine villages in Switzerland and Austria construct concrete or stone barriers in the form of an upsidedown V on the slopes above. In the event of an avalanche, these act as splitting wedges that steer the snow to either side and away from the villages below.

Nations throughout the world employ snowsheds to protect motorists on highways from avalanches. These tunnel-like concrete roofs built over highways allow avalanche snows to slide over the highway without harming traffic.

Steel snow fences and other artificial barriers provide some protection to villages that lie in unstable areas.

Education

The combination of preventive avalanche triggering, refined methods of passive protection, and more thorough weather forecasting that warns people of increased avalanche potential has greatly increased safety in many avalanche zones. In the United States, recreation-area and highway personnel have become so effective in performing their jobs that fewer than 1 percent of the nation's avalanche fatalities occur on open ski runs or on mountain roads.

At the same time, however, the number of avalanche fatalities in the country has been growing steadily. The reason has been the increased number of uninformed recreationists who venture into remote avalanche territory. Many of them have no idea of what avalanches are, how they are caused, or how they can be avoided. Trying to educate such people about the dangers they face has been a continuous job. No sooner did experts devise ways of keeping ski slopes safe than back-country skiers began running into problems. After an aggressive education program cut back on backcountry ski accidents, snowmobilers began invading remote areas with sometimes tragic results. "Each time a new recreational group comes along, they have to learn about avalanches the hard way,"[47] says Bruce Tremper.

Keeping the Passes Clear

Because of the number of people they carry into and through avalanche country, highways and railroads that cut through mountain passes are among the most dangerous places to be when heavy snows are falling. Rogers Pass in British Columbia, Canada, has long been one of the world's most treacherous transportation zones. Both a major railway and Canada's main national highway, which links the cities of Vancouver and Calgary, wind through the steep, snow-choked mountains of this pass. The twenty-five-mile route crosses more than 130 regular avalanche paths. David Skjonsberg, a Parks Canada highway manager, estimates that, since construction of the railroad in 1885, more than two hundred people have died from avalanches there.

In 1974 a large avalanche destroyed a service station, motel, and coffee shop in the area. This prompted a concentrated effort to control avalanches on British Columbia's highways, and particularly in Rogers Pass. Concrete bunkers were built to protect stretches of highway, and gullies were carved out to divert avalanche paths. Currently a group of eleven experts monitor avalanche conditions and bombard the mountains with explosives to keep the snowpack from building up to treacherous conditions. On rare occasions when the weather is clear, they drop explosives from helicopters onto the remote slopes. At all other times, they fire 2.2-pound explosive chargers from howitzers placed in a series of towers located out of harm's way.

Despite their best efforts to keep the traffic flowing, authorities have to close the highway to traffic for an average of 160 hours each winter. They have accomplished their main objective, however: Since 1976, no avalanche fatalities have occurred at Rogers Pass or along any other British Columbia highway.

U.S. forest rangers can often see disaster coming but are powerless to stop it. Because many of the best backcountry ski and snowmobile areas are on public lands, the rangers cannot deny entry even when avalanche conditions are extreme. "Even if we're 99 percent sure a guy will get killed, we have to let him in,"[48] says Rogers Thompson of the U.S. Forest Service.

Experts agree that the best way to limit the effects of avalanches is for people to become informed about them. "Many more lives will be saved by education, avalanche control works, and precautionary measures than will be saved by rescuers,"[49] says Atkins. Yet the burden of educating the public has become more difficult in many areas of the world due to funding cutbacks. In the United States, government facilities in Alaska and Colorado have recently been eliminated. As a result, research on avalanches is largely confined to projects in Switzerland, Japan, and Canada.

Taking Risks

Given the unpredictability of avalanches and their devastating potential for destruction, the only sure way of preventing them from inflicting tragedy is to stay clear of them. However, avalanches occur precisely where outdoor recreationists like to be. The thirty-five-degree slopes that run the greatest risk of an avalanche are the very slopes that make the best expert ski runs. The remote powder slopes that are ideal for snowmobiling and the high mountains that challenge the skills of climbers are prime avalanche territory.

Outdoor recreationists are willing to assume a degree of risk in pursuit of their interests. "In my opinion [safe mountaineering] is meaningless," writes Russian climber Vladimir Shatayev. "One might as well remove the oxygen from a molecule of water and call the remainder water."[50] People such as Shatayev understand that there is a risk of injury or death in their sport, but they are willing to assume that risk.

But when recreationists invest an enormous amount of time, money, and effort in pursuit of their sport, they may be especially reluctant to abandon a day's outing even when they know better. A U.S. mountain climber whose group flirted with danger climbing Russia's tallest mountain, Lenin Peak, in 1987, later explained the decision to keep going when their snow-pit tests revealed an unstable snowpack like this: "Probably without being fully aware of it, some of us may have thought 'How can we turn back, after coming all this way to Russia?'"[51]

However, experienced outdoor enthusiasts do not allow the thirst for adventure and excitement or even fulfillment of long-held dreams to override safety precautions. "No professional I have ever met has any patience with or respect for daredevils,"[52] says Monty Atwater. Such people not only put themselves at risk but also threaten the lives of those called on to rescue them.

Mountain climbers and other sports enthusiasts sometimes flirt with disaster in the pursuit of their sport.

Avoiding Avalanches

According to experts, dangerous avalanches can be avoided most of the time. The first step in any outdoor winter adventure is to contact local ski areas, mountain guides, and government authorities to learn of any warnings about local avalanche conditions. Next, accurate weather information for the time in which one is to be out should be obtained. The safest rule is to stay off the slopes during periods of heavy snow and for twenty-four hours after such snow or after periods of prolonged high winds.

Once out in the mountains, the safest procedure is to stay on established trails. If that is not possible, dangerous terrain such as slopes of thirty to forty-five degrees and steep-sided bowls and canyons should be avoided. "The safest place to travel," writes Robert Young Pelton, "is along the valley floor away from large avalanche run-outs, along ridgetops above avalanche paths, in dense timber, or on slopes of 25 degrees or less with no steep slopes above them."[53] It is also best to stay to the windblown side of any ridge.

During group activities in the winter mountains, it is essential to have a leader who not only understands the dangers of avalanches but also exercises good judgment and knows when to turn back. But even experienced mountain guides sometimes fail to keep their charges out of harm's way. One guide, supposedly experienced in winter moun-

Hidden Patrol

Many people were surprised when the International Olympic Committee awarded the 1960 Winter Olympics to a remote and obscure resort area of California known as Squaw Valley. No one was more surprised than avalanche experts, who noted that the slopes being used for this event lay directly in some of the most dangerous avalanche country in the world. With thousands of participants and spectators roaming these unstable slopes, Squaw Valley seemed a disaster in the making.

Olympic officials called on avalanche expert Monty Atwater to keep the snowpack under control. Before and during the games, Atwater and six teams of assistants blasted away at the slopes with four 75-millimeter guns and two 105-millimeter recoilless rifles. Under enormous pressure to prevent a disaster, Atwater and his group worked every morning to clear the slopes of danger before the day's activity. In the process, they developed several new methods of explosive avalanche control, such as dropping bombs from ski lifts and using shells with delayed fuses.

The effort was a complete success. Not one person was hurt in an avalanche at Squaw Valley. Even more remarkable, although Atwater's crews triggered a total of 137 slides, few visitors to the Olympics were aware that there was any avalanche control going on.

tain hiking, led nine French schoolchildren and a teacher to their deaths on a hiking trip in the Alps in 1998. In the aftermath of the tragedy, experts concluded that in deciding to use that route on that day, the guide had shown astoundingly bad judgment. In February 2001 seven men traveling in the mountains of Tajikistan paid the ultimate price for their poor judgment. They decided to risk driving on a remote road that had been closed for the winter for safety reasons. They lost their gamble when a massive avalanche buried them in their car.

Dangerous Encroachments

Avalanches have become an increasing danger not only because of individual outdoor recreationists heading for the mountains but also because of the encroachment of communities. As resort towns and chalets climb higher into what were once considered uninhabitable regions of the mountains, the same avalanches that once fell harmlessly can now create major problems.

In the Alps the steady expansion of ski facilities has contributed to a series of deadly disasters. During peak holiday seasons, some of these areas become as densely populated as a city. When avalanches fall on these locations, the devastation can be appalling. On February 10, 1970, a massive avalanche killed thirty-nine people at Avon Val d'Isere in France, which was built in the 1930s directly in an avalanche zone. During the terrible winter of 1998–99, more than four dozen people were killed and many more injured in chalets and villages built in high-risk avalanche zones. Many thousands of tourists were stranded by deep snows and had to be evacuated by military helicopters.

A similarly dangerous encroachment of development into avalanche territory has been occurring within the United States. Expansion of construction in mountain areas has increased dramatically, bringing thousands of people within range of avalanche problems. Developers in Keystone, Colorado, alone, have plans for building seventeen hundred single-family homes

As development moves into high mountain areas, the risk of avalanche disasters grows.

and condominiums within the next five years. Forested slopes have been cleared to make way for ski resorts and communities in dozens of previously uninhabited regions of the western mountains.

The development of land in avalanche zones has begun to alarm some observers. In recent years Switzerland has strictly enforced prohibitions on construction within avalanche zones. Following the rash of avalanche disasters in 1999, Eva Liechtenberger, a local Austrian government official, noted, "It should be a warning to us to think again about what we are doing in the high mountains."[54] According to Colorado's avalanche information director, Knox Williams, "We don't have the narrow, heavily inhabited valleys of the Alps. But if there is enough of this expansion of home sites, we will start to see this problem in this country."[55]

The degree to which governments will restrict construction in avalanche zones is yet to be determined. At the present time the lure of the scenic mountains, with their pristine white-coated slopes, remains strong and all but guarantees that the White Death of the high mountains will visit with increasing frequency.

Notes

Introduction: The White Death

1. Quoted in British Broadcasting Corporation, "Anatomy of an Avalanche," November 25, 1999. www.bbc.co.uk.

2. Quoted in Public Broadcasting System transcript, "Killer Avalanches," February 25, 1999. www.pbs.org/newshour.

Chapter One: Snow Falling Down Mountains

3. Quoted in David Cupp, "Winter's White Death," *National Geographic,* September 1982, p. 290.

4. Quoted in Cupp, "Winter's White Death," p. 290.

5. Quoted in Colin Fraser, *Avalanches and Snow Safety.* New York: Charles Scribner's Sons, 1978, p. 41.

Chapter Two: What Causes an Avalanche?

6. Quoted in Fraser, *Avalanches and Snow Safety*, p. 42.

7. Quoted in McKay Jenkins, *The White Death.* New York: Random House, 2000, p. 14.

8. Yvon Chouinard, *Climbing Ice*. San Francisco: Sierra Club Books, 1978, p. 161.

9. Quoted in Mary Neareth, "When the Snow Turns Treacherous," *Maclean's*, April 24, 1994, p. 54.

10. U.S. Forest Service National Avalanche Center, "Is the Snowpack Unstable?" www.avalanche.org/~nac.

11. Chouinard, *Climbing Ice*, p. 163.

12. Chouinard, *Climbing Ice*, p. 165.

13. Quoted in Jenkins, *The White Death*, p.74.

14. Eileen Gallagher, *The Insider's Guide to Glacier*. Helena, MT: Falcon, 1999, p. 143

15. Quoted in Neareth, "When the Snow Turns Treacherous," p. 54.

Chapter Three: Predicting Avalanches

16. Bill Birkett, *Modern Rock and Ice Climbing*. London: A&C Burke, 1988, p. 20.

17. Quoted in Vivien Bowers, "Starting a Slide for Safety's Sake," *Canadian Geographic*, March 1994, p. 22.

18. Chouinard, *Climbing Ice*, p. 163.

19. Chouinard, *Climbing Ice*, p. 160.

20. Bruce Tremper, "Popular Myths About Avalanches." www.avalanche.org/~nac.

21. LaSal Avalanche Forecasting Center, "Avalanche Awareness Tutorial." www.avalanche.org/~lsafac.

22. Candace Burns and Jo Dearbrouck, *The Insiders' Guide to Yellowstone*. Manteo, NC: Insiders', 1998, p. 427.

23. LaSal Avalanche Forecasting Center, "Avalanche Awareness Tutorial."

24. Quoted in Neareth, "When the Snow Turns Treacherous," p. 54.

Chapter Four: A Close-Up View of an Avalanche

25. Jenkins, *The White Death*, p. 159.

26. Quoted in J. Madeline Nash, "Eluding the White Death," *Time*, March 8, 1993, p. 61.

27. Quoted in Kari Grady Grossman, "Winter Kills," 1999. www.discovery.com/exp/avalanche.

28. Peter Lew, "Anatomy of an Avalanche," *Avalanche Review*, January 1987. www.avalanche.org/%7Emoonstone.

29. Quoted in Ryan Kuhn, "Golden Snowmobilers Caught in Avalanche Lucky to Be Alive," *Golden Star*, March

26, 2001. www.csac.org/incidents/2000-1.

30. Quoted in *New York Times*, "Search Opens After Avalanche Kills at Least Ten in French Alps," February 11, 1999, p. A-11.

31. Quoted in *New York Times*, "Search Opens After Avalanche Kills at Least Ten in French Alps," p. A-11.

32. Quoted in Bowers, "Starting a Slide for Safety's Sake," p. 22.

33. Quoted in Bart McDowell, "Avalanche!" *National Geographic*, June 1962, p. 855.

Chapter Five: Survival and Rescue

34. Robert Young Pelton, *Come Back Alive*. New York: Doubleday, 1999, p. 74.

35. Quoted in Jenkins, *The White Death*, p. 51.

36. Chouinard, *Climbing Ice*, p. 160.

37. Pelton, *Come Back Alive*, p. 74.

38. Quoted in LaSal Avalanche Forecasting Center, "Avalanche Awareness Tutorial."

39. Dale Atkins, "Mistakes in Avalanche Rescues," *Avalanche Review*, April 1991. www.avalanche.org/%7Emoonstone.

40. John Hart, *Walking Softly in the Wilderness*. San Francisco: Sierra Club Books, 1977, p. 292.

41. Atkins, "Mistakes in Avalanche Rescues."

42. Atkins, "Mistakes in Avalanche Rescues."

43. Atkins, "Mistakes in Avalanche Rescues."

44. Quoted in Brian E. Clark, "Breaking Away: Avalanche Dogs Are Life-Savers Happy to Serve," *Modesto Bee,* February 9, 1999. www.modbee.com/sports/story.

45. Quoted in Clark, "Breaking Away."

Chapter Six: Living with Avalanches

46. Quoted in James Brooke, "U.S. Avalanche Experts See Future Threat in Rockies," *New York Times,* February 25, 1999, p. A-10.

47. Tremper, "Popular Myths About Avalanches."

48. Quoted in Cupp, "Winter's White Death," p. 304.

49. Atkins, "Mistakes in Avalanche Rescues."

50. Vladimir Shatayev, *Degrees of Difficulty*. Seattle: Mountaineers, 1987, p. 136.

51. Lew, "Anatomy of an Avalanche."

52. Quoted in Jenkins, *The White Death*, p. 68.

53. Pelton, *Come Back Alive*, p. 74.

54. Quoted in John Hooper et al., "Undeterred Britons Head for Slopes of Death," *London Guardian*, February 28, 1999. www.guardian.co.uk/weather.

55. Quoted in Brooke, "U.S. Avalanche Experts See Future Threat in Rockies," p. A-10.

Glossary

avalanche: Snow cover that falls or slides down a slope over a distance greater than 50 meters, or 165 feet, about the width of a football field.

binding: The characteristic of sticking together or clinging that occurs between individual snowflakes and between layers of a snowpack.

chute: The path that an avalanche takes as it slides down a slope.

cornice: A drift created when wind piles snow onto a ridge, forming an overhang of densely packed snow that may jut out many feet from the actual rock. This unsupported weight leaves it vulnerable to breaking off and tumbling down a slope.

hoar: A thin layer of frost or frozen moisture.

loose-snow avalanche: A snowslide in which the layer or layers of snow that slide do not hold together as they fall but rather pour down like a pile of sugar.

passive protection: Immobile structures designed to shield an area from the effects of a natural disaster such as an avalanche.

runout zone: The area at the bottom of a slope where an avalanche comes to rest.

shear: To cut loose a portion (of a snowpack, for example), often with a sharp-edged object such as a shovel.

slab avalanche: A snowslide in which a layer or layers of snow temporarily hold together as the snow releases from the slope, falling as a series of chunks or slabs.

sluff: A small, loose snowslide that is almost never dangerous.

snowpack: The accumulation of snow on the ground. It may contain many layers of snow from various snowfalls.

sugar snow: A common expression for snow that does not pack or bind but rather acts much like a pile of sugar.

For Further Reading

Books

Peter H. Goodwin, *Landslides, Slumps, and Creep*. New York: Franklin Watts, 1997. A short, readable, well-illustrated description of the causes and consequences of landslides and snowslides.

John Marshall, *Living (and Dying) in Avalanche Country*. Silverton, Colorado: Simpler Way Book Company, 1993. Stories of avalanches in the San Juan Mountains of Colorado told by local citizens who lived through them.

Buck Tilton, *Avalanche Safety*. Guilford, CT: Globe Pequot, 1993. A teacher of wilderness medicine details how to avoid getting injured in an avalanche.

Periodicals

David Goodman, "When the Mountain Falls," *Outside*, February 2000.

Valerie Marchant, "Steep, Deep, and Deadly," *Time*, March 8, 1999.

National Geographic World, "Avalanche," January 1997.

Works Consulted

Books

Bill Birkett, *Modern Rock and Ice Climbing*. London: A&C Burke, 1988. Although most of the book discusses climbing techniques, a section on dealing with avalanches is included.

Candace Burns and Jo Dearbrouck, *The Insiders' Guide to Yellowstone*. Manteo, NC: Insiders', 1998. A basic user's guide to the national park and brief tips on coping with avalanches.

Yvon Chouinard, *Climbing Ice*. San Francisco: Sierra Club Books, 1978. One of the foremost winter climbers devotes a section to practical advice regarding avalanches.

Colin Fraser, *Avalanches and Snow Safety*. New York: Charles Scribner's Sons, 1978. One of the acknowledged experts on avalanches includes fascinating history along with current information.

Eileen Gallagher, *The Insider's Guide to Glacier*. Helena, MT: Falcon, 1999. Another basic user's guide.

John Hart, *Walking Softly in the Wilderness*. San Francisco: Sierra Club Books, 1977. More poetic than other books dealing with the outdoors.

McKay Jenkins, *The White Death*. New York: Random House, 2000. By far the most fascinating and complete treatment of avalanches.

Robert Young Pelton, *Come Back Alive*. New York: Doubleday, 1999. This practical guide to surviving a vast range of disasters includes a section on avalanches.

Vladimir Shatayev, *Degrees of Difficulty*. Seattle: Mountaineers, 1987. A veteran Russian mountaineer whose wife died in a climbing accident describes the risks and benefits of winter recreation.

Periodicals

Vivien Bowers, "Starting a Slide for Safety's Sake," *Canadian Geographic*, March 1994.

James Brooke, "U.S. Avalanche Experts See Future Threat in Rockies," *New York Times*, February 25, 1999.

David Cupp, "Winter's White Death," *National Geographic*, September 1982.

Bart McDowell, "Avalanche!" *National Geographic,* June 1962.

J. Madeline Nash, "Eluding the White Death," *Time*, March 8, 1993.

Mary Neareth, "When the Snow Turns Treacherous," *Maclean's*, April 24, 1994.

New York Times, "Search Opens After Avalanche Kills at Least Ten in French Alps," February 11, 1999.

Internet Sources

Dale Atkins, "Mistakes in Avalanche Rescues," *Avalanche Review*, April 1991. www.avalanche.org/%7Emoonstone.

British Broadcasting Corporation, "Anatomy of an Avalanche," November 25, 1999. www.bbc.co.uk.

Brian E. Clark, "Breaking Away: Avalanche Dogs Are Life-Savers Happy to Serve," *Modesto Bee*, February 9, 1999. www.modbee.com/sports/story.

Kari Grady Grossman, "Winter Kills," 1999. www.discovery. com/exp/avalanche.

John Hooper et al., "Undeterred Britons Head for Slopes of Death," *London Guardian*, February 28, 1999. www.guardian. co.uk/weather.

Ryan Kuhn, "Golden Snowmobilers Caught in Avalanche Lucky to Be Alive," *Golden Star*, March 26, 2001. www.csac.org/ incidents/2000-1.

LaSal Avalanche Forecasting Center, "Avalanche Awareness Tutorial." www.avalanche.org/~lsafac.

Peter Lew, "Anatomy of an Avalanche," *Avalanche Review,* January 1987. www.avalanche.org/%7Emoonstone.

Public Broadcasting System, "Killer Avalanches," February 25, 1999. www.pbs.org/newshour.

Jan Reuter, "Snowmobiler Dies in Avalanche," *Summit County Daily News*, April 3, 2001. www.csac.org/incidents/2000-1.

Bruce Tremper, "Popular Myths About Avalanches." www. avalanche.org/~nac.

U.S. Forest Service National Avalanche Center, "Is the Snow-pack Unstable?" www.avalanche.org/~nac.

Index

Picture Credits

About the Author

Nathan Aaseng is the author of more than 160 books on a wide range of subjects. Aaseng, an avid cross-country skier from Eau Claire, Wisconsin, was a 1999 recipient of the Wisconsin Library Association's Notable Author Award.